# Steely Dan

## *the* Complete Guide *to their* Music

OMNIBUS PRESS
London/New York
Paris/Sydney/Copenhagen
Berlin/Madrid/Tokyo

Brian Sweet

Copyright © 1998 & 2004 Omnibus Press
(A Division of Book Sales Limited)

Cover and book designed by Chloë Alexander
Picture research by Sarah Bacon

ISBN: 1.84449.425.X
Order No: OP50248

Exclusive Distributors
Book Sales Limited
8/9 Frith Street,
London W1D 3JB, UK.

Music Sales Corporation
257 Park Avenue South,
New York, NY 10010, USA.

Music Sales Pty Limited,
120 Rothschild Avenue, Rosebery,
NSW 2018, Australia.

To the Music Trade only:
Music Sales Limited,
8/9 Frith Street,
London W1D 3JB, UK.

Every effort has been made to trace the copyright holders
of the photographs in this book but one or two were
unreachable. We would be grateful if the photographers
concerned would contact us.

Printed by Mackays of Chatham plc, Chatham, Kent

A catalogue record for this book is available from the
British Library.

Visit Omnibus Press at http://www.musicsales.co.uk

# Contents

INTRODUCTION 4

Can't Buy A Thrill 8
Countdown To Ecstasy 12
Pretzel Logic 17
Katy Lied 22
The Royal Scam 27
Aja 32
Gaucho 36
Two Against Nature 40
Everything Must Go 44

DONALD FAGEN
Nightfly 40
Kamakiriad 51

WALTER BECKER
Eleven Tracks Of Whack 55

Compilations & Miscellaneous 59

Outside Projects 73

Index 78

# INTRODUCTION

**S**TEELY **D**AN WERE THE ULTIMATE STUDIO BAND OF THE SEVENTIES. THEY CAME together in 1972, formed around the songwriting partnership of Donald Fagen and Walter Becker, two self-confessed wiseass New Yorkers who shared an interest in bebop jazz and Beat literature. Becker and Fagen were total control freaks who were at their most comfortable on leather couches in windowless, air-conditioned recording studios where everything – especially the music – could be controlled.

As Steely Dan's career progressed they spent ever more time and money in studios crafting songs for their albums. Becker and Fagen thought nothing of trying all the songs on an album with six or seven different bands and/or different combinations of crack session players painstakingly attempting to play the composition to their incredibly exacting standards. If, by then, they had failed to get a satisfactory basic track they would more than likely shelve the song completely. Nothing half-baked or half-assed passed their quality control.

Between 1972 and 1980, Steely Dan released seven studio albums of an amazingly high standard; no, they didn't provide quantity, but, by God, they certainly provided quality. This was borne out by the fact that *Can't Buy A Thrill*, *Countdown To Ecstasy*, *Pretzel Logic*, *Katy Lied* and *The Royal Scam* all went gold and the subsequent two, *Aja* and *Gaucho*, went platinum. In 1978 they released a *Greatest Hits* package which went platinum. This contained the previously unreleased song 'Here At The Western World,' which attested to the strength of material they would frequently leave off their studio albums.

Becker and Fagen first met in 1967 at Bard College in upstate New York. Walter Becker was only seventeen at the time, but had taken guitar lessons from an even younger kid called Randy Wolfe (later to be rechristened Randy California, and to become founder member of Spirit), who in turn had been taught by his stepfather Ed Cassidy. They became firm friends and were soon writing songs together and forming bands on the campus. The Don Fagen Jazz Trio might play at a charity night, The Leather Canary might play in the Red Balloon (the college coffee house) and The Bad Rock Group might be engaged for the Halloween party. One line-up featured comedian Chevy Chase on drums.

In 1969, Fagen graduated as an English major but Becker had already been asked to leave for neglecting his studies. They moved to New York City and rather naively began trying to sell their self-confessed "cheesy" songs to music publishers. One day they met Kenny Vance, a member of Jay & The Americans, in the Brill Building where JATA had a publishing company. At this point Becker and Fagen didn't even have a demo tape, and were waltzing into offices with their exercise book of lyrics under their arms, sitting down at the omnipresent piano, and singing their songs to anyone prepared to listen.

Vance liked a couple of their songs and offered them a publishing deal, and they began recording demos at various Manhattan studios. This was a step in the right direction, but it didn't provide the two songwriters with any income. Becker and Fagen were living hand to mouth out in Brooklyn, and to help his protegés to pay the rent, Vance also hired them as backing musicians for Jay & The Americans, who had had a number of hits in the early to mid-Sixties, but were now reduced to playing oldies shows on the east coast. Although this offered regular employment, Becker and Fagen were never ones to rest on their laurels and they answered an ad in the *Village Voice* that sought "a bass player and keyboard player with jazz chops". The ad had been placed by a guitarist named Denny Dias who lived in Hicksville, Long Island. Becker and Fagen liked Denny, and Denny and lead singer Keith Thomas were amazed by the intensity and weirdness of their songs. Becker and Fagen were not really interested in the group, which was more or less a covers group, as they wanted to play their own material, but they did enlist Dias and Thomas's help in recording demos, which Vance produced.

Months, indeed years, went by without much headway being made, although Vance did secure them some paid work writing a film score for a low-budget movie which was being made by a young independent filmmaker named Peter Locke. The soundtrack album to the film was eventually released in 1978 to cash in on Steely Dan's success.

As their list of contacts expanded, Becker and Fagen befriended another independent record producer, Gary Kannon (who was to later change his name to Katz). When in 1971 he was offered a job in Los Angeles as a staff producer at ABC Records, he rang Becker and Fagen and invited them to join him out there – ostensibly as staff writers for the burgeoning underground music label. They packed up and left New York, leaving Vance high and dry, and in order to be released from their contract with him, they eventually gave him half the publishing on their debut album.

Once settled in California, Becker and Fagen were given an office with a piano where they began writing songs for ABC artists such as The Grass Roots, Tommy Roe and Three Dog Night. They wrote a song called 'Tell Me A Lie' for The Grass Roots but it was never recorded – in fact none of their efforts ever made it to vinyl. Although Becker and Fagen had no problem with the melodies or harmonies, they couldn't help inserting a weird angle to the lyrics. After six months of continual rejection and frustration, they called some of their friends back east and asked them to come to California and start a band so that they could record some of their unrecorded material. With Denny Dias, Jeff Baxter and Jim Hodder on board, Steely Dan was born – the name taken from a steam-powered dildo in William Burroughs' *The Naked Lunch*.

Starting out as a five-piece, quickly expanding to six members, then gradually declining in size until only Becker and Fagen remained, Steely Dan was simply a vehicle for the duo to drive their songs into the audience's consciousness, there to remain like some treasured old memory. The outstanding thing about most Becker and Fagen songs is their longevity; there's so much going on musically and lyrically that one never tires of hearing them.

Although legend often paints a different picture, between late 1972 and mid-1974, Steely Dan did do stints on the road, promoting their albums around America. However, the experience was so disagreeable (particularly for Fagen) that after a gig at the Santa Monica Civic Auditorium they announced with some relief their retirement from touring. Not until 1993 were they seen live again under the Steely Dan banner, having reformed the band concept with a fresh bunch of musicians.

By the time they recorded their third album, Becker and Fagen were being encouraged by their friend and producer Gary Katz to adopt a workshop situation whereby they would use the most suitable studio player for a particular part. Of course, using these session men was a very expensive way to record an album, but as Fagen once said "We usually spare no expense," even though in the long run the cost of the album would be deducted from their royalties. (*Gaucho* is reputed to have cost a million dollars.) By then Steely Dan had become victims of their own attainment, trying to surpass their most successful album *Aja* both creatively and saleswise.

Becker and Fagen's 14 year partnership was under great strain for a variety of personal reasons, and in June 1981, they announced a split – at least for the time being. Becker moved to Hawaii to start a new life and, although collaborating on a few songs in the mid-Eighties, they did not perform together again until 1992. The idea was to play some of their favourite Sixties soul songs written by Bert Berns and Jerry Ragavoy alongside the occasional Steely Dan song. The audience response to the Steely Dan material was so heartening that Becker and Fagen felt obliged to return a couple of years later and offer a show of exclusive Dan songs.

Between 1972 and 1980 Steely Dan had ten Top 40 US singles, while only one reached a comparable level in the UK. Oddly enough, that one, the reggae influenced "Haitian Divorce", wasn't even released as a single in America. All their studio albums except *Countdown To Ecstasy* went Top 30 in America, with *Aja* by far the most successful, peaking at No 3 in 1977.

A year after Becker and Fagen split the band in 1981, Donald Fagen released *The Nightfly* to much critical acclaim, using the same nucleus of players as Steely Dan, with Gary Katz producing. After its release, Fagen suffered from a writer's block which lasted for the rest of the decade, a period he spent lying low in New York. He filled in his time by writing an occasional satirical column in the film magazine *Premier*, and doodling around with 'fun' projects such as writing a couple of songs for an animator friend, the odd film song ('The Companion' for *Heavy Metal* and 'The Finer Things' for Martin Scorsese's *King Of Comedy*), as well as a few songs for Diana Ross and Yellow Jackets. Meanwhile, from his base in Miami, Walter Becker started dabbling again, producing a couple of albums for China Crisis and one by the lightweight Norwegian band Fra Lippo Lippi.

In the early Nineties, Fagen married Libby Titus who had once been married to Levon Helm from The Band, and it was she who eventually encouraged him to go out and play live again. Being a fan of soul music, Fagen put together a sort of ongoing tribute to the songwriting team of Bert Berns and Jerry Ragavoy. It got him back on creative track and in 1993 he released a second solo album, *Kamakiriad*.

In 1997, Becker and Fagen were in a studio in Maui working on a new Steely Dan studio album, the first since 1980's *Gaucho*. During their 1996 US tour they actually previewed three new songs ('Jack Of Speed', 'Cash Only Island' and 'Wet Side Story') but only the first of these found its way on to the album *Two Against Nature* which finally came out in February 2000. With new material to promote, Steely Dan toured extensively in America, Japan and Europe. Becker and Fagen were truly on a roll: in summer 2003, a follow-up *Everything Must Go* hit the stores, but sales of the latter paled into insignificance compared with its predecessor and, while in 1993, Steely Dan had played Madison Square Garden, ten years later they were relegated to the Roseland ballroom.

Now both in their mid-fifties, Becker and Fagen's powers of influence are seemingly on the wane. Indeed, there was considerable speculation that the song 'Everything Must Go' surreptitiously spelt a "second end" for Steely Dan. Though no announcement has yet been made, Fagen is reportedly writing and recording the final part of a trilogy to round off The *Nightfly* and *Kamakiriad*. Whatever may lie in the future for Walter Becker and Donald Fagen, Steely Dan's original seven-album career assures them of their place alongside the greats in rock history.

# Can't Buy A Thrill

Probe SPB 1062, January 1973; reissued as ABC ABCL 5034,
October 1974; current LP MCA MCL 1769 (1983) CD MCAD 37040 (1983)

**W**HEN STEELY DAN ENTERED THE RECORDING STUDIO IN THE LATE SUMMER OF 1972, the five hastily assembled members had yet to actually play a gig together. The two principal members, Walter Becker and Donald Fagen, were failed staff songwriters at ABC Dunhill who had spent the previous six months trying to convince both themselves and the powers-that-be at ABC that they could write hit songs for the roster of artists there at the time.

The pair secured a recording deal of their own, rehearsed in the ABC offices after hours, and went into the Village Recorder in Santa Monica to make an album (they had by this time already issued a single called 'Dallas' which flopped). Joining Becker and Fagen were another group of transplanted east coasters; their old buddy guitarist Denny Dias, Jeff "Skunk" Baxter also on guitar and casual acquaintance Jim Hodder on drums.

Even while recording the album, unanimously elected singer Donald Fagen was uncomfortable in the lead vocal role and the band tried to find an alternative. Becker and Fagen later said what they were really looking for was an actor to assume the role of singer, and they eventually came up with David Palmer, much to the annoyance of producer Gary Katz, who argued against the decision on a daily basis.

By the time *Can't Buy A Thrill* was released in the US, Steely Dan were out on the road supporting a succession of artists, including Elton John, The Kinks, The Beach Boys and The James Gang. Meanwhile, radio programmes had picked up on the opening song 'Do It Again' and given it heavy rotation, so in early 1973 ABC put it out as a single, and it became a top ten hit, reaching No 6 in the *Billboard* chart. A couple of months later Steely Dan put out 'Reelin' In The Years', a follow-up single which charted at number 11, providing them with a supercharged start to their career.

The band's original idea for a cover concept featured a young girl looking in a porn shop window while the owner leered at her from inside. A photo shoot with Gary Katz's daughter actually took place, but the band thought better of it. ABC's idea for the cover – a collage dominated by French prostitutes, didn't please Steely Dan at all, but by then it was too late to change it. Unbeknown to critics and fans alike, Becker and Fagen wrote the sleeve notes themselves, using an old pseudonym from their Jay & The Americans days – Tristan Fabriani.

Becker and Fagen took the title for the album from the opening lines of the Bob Dylan song, 'It Takes A Lot To Laugh, It Takes A Train To Cry' – "Well I ride on a mail train baby/Can't buy a thrill" – from his 1965 LP *Highway 61 Revisited*.

Donald Fagen would later term most of the album "juvenilia", but in 1972 Steely Dan were a real, working, touring band and the album retains the freshness and enthusiasm of young men embarking on their musical career full of hopes and dreams.

## DO IT AGAIN

THE OPENING song on Steely Dan's début was almost six minutes long, and told a tale of betrayal, random violence and revenge – all regular subjects for future Becker/Fagen compositions. Sung by the none-too-keen Donald Fagen in his own inimitable style, this minor key spaghetti western was edited down for a single and promptly went Top Ten in the US *Billboard* chart in early 1973. Despite heavy airplay, it didn't chart in the UK until 1975. Producer Gary Katz later admitted that they had no idea that it was a hit single. By Becker and Fagen's standards, the song was written very quickly. The duo liked the vocal sound on the cut, which was achieved by putting the signal through a device called a Cooper Time Tube. Although they tried to achieve the same effect on later tracks, they never succeeded.

The two fastidious songwriters were looking for a drone in the background of the song, but when they were unable to find an acoustic sitar anywhere they settled on an electric one played by Denny Dias. The Steely Dan of the future would not give up so easily once they had a particular effect in mind.

## DIRTY WORK

HAVING hired ex-Quinaimes and Jake & The Family Jewels singer David Palmer when the album was almost finished, Becker and Fagen provided him with this uncomplicated pop song which suited his vocal style much better than their usual ironic, slightly subversive material. Jerome Richardson played the tenor solo. On the surface the song seemed sugary and sentimental, and was later covered by all-girl group Birtha, Ian Matthews and José Feliciano. A closer listen reveals a man who is so utterly infatuated with someone else's woman that when her regular partner is unavailable, he will run to her at the snap of her fingers.

## KINGS

DESCRIBED by Becker and Fagen as a "vacuous historical romance", 'Kings' featured a guitar solo by Elliott Randall which was intended to be a "deliberate trip into schizophrenia land" lurching from the very melodic to extremely obtuse and back again; and which Randall claimed reflected his troubled personal life at the time.

The song outlines the life of a glory seeker with an unquenchable blood lust and his blinkered disciples who follow him into battle come-what-may. Fagen's voice is thick with urgency as are the female backing vocals.

## MIDNITE CRUISER

'MIDNITE Cruiser' was another old song which Becker and Fagen decided was worthy of recording for their debut album. Jim Hodder had already sung the lead vocal on the melancholy 'Dallas', and when he offered to sing this one Becker and Fagen rapidly agreed. In the US, the album was released in a gatefold sleeve complete with lyrics, and on the lyric sheet the character's name is spelt as 'Felonius', but Hodder definitely pronounces it 'Thelonious', a sly reference to jazz pianist Thelonius Monk, a firm Becker and Fagen favourite. Fagen surely had his tongue in cheek when explaining that the song was about the late nights spent on the street in New York City where he and Becker witnessed some very strange behaviour and felonious characters.

The song inspired sci-fi writer William Gibson to name a bar 'The Gentleman Loser' in his cyberpunk novel *Neuromancer*.

Becker and Fagen dusted this song off during the 1996 Steely Dan world tour, with Walter Becker taking the lead vocal. However, his rather gruff performance ensured that it was stripped from the set list.

## ONLY A FOOL WOULD SAY THAT

BECKER and Fagen often said that at the start of their career they didn't know what they wanted to do, and that consequently *Can't Buy a Thrill* was a mixture of styles. After the upbeat 'Midnite Cruiser', the Latin influenced 'Only A Fool Would Say That', with its shuffling beat, sprinkling percussion and jazzy guitar, brings the listener back down to earth with a story of a man who is numb to all the cruel happenings in the world.

Jeff "Skunk" Baxter, who had spent some of his formative years in Mexico City, spoke the line of Spanish at the end of the song.

## REELIN' IN THE YEARS

'REELIN' In The Years' provided Steely Dan with their second hit single in early 1973. The guitar solo, purely by accident, fell to Elliott Randall – he was visiting the studio on the day they were trying to record the solo and Jeff Baxter, having been unable to nail it himself, nobly suggested that Elliott should try it. (It's reputedly Jimmy Page's all-time favourite guitar solo.)

On this track, Becker and Fagen got the musical idea first, and later added the lyrics, which detail a lack of understanding between two lovers. She really doesn't know a good thing when she's got it.

Fagen's tongue curls around each syllable and effortlessly fires them out like an automatic weapon, while Becker's bass follows the piano part, bounding up and down the scale and behind the six-part harmonies on the chorus.

## FIRE IN THE HOLE

YET ANOTHER old song, but this one's weirder than all the others put together. Borrowing a phrase used by American soldiers in the Vietnam war to describe when a grenade was thrown down into a camouflaged hide in a Vietcong village, Becker and Fagen spin a tale of a returned veteran who is now bordering on insanity. Kicking off with Fagen's insistent piano intro, his piano solo leads into Jeff Baxter's pedal steel guitar, which soothes the listener into the fade.

## BROOKLYN (OWES THE CHARMER UNDER ME)

WRITTEN while Donald Fagen was living on President Street in Brooklyn, Steely Dan dedicated this song to 'President Street Pete' (who lived in the apartment below him) for "all the indignity he had to suffer, sitting on the stoop and

shooting the shit about the Mets" for years. It provided David Palmer with his second vocal, and Jeff Baxter with another chance to demonstrate his prowess on pedal steel guitar. Becker and Fagen had demoed the song years earlier with Kenny Vance, but this was a much more sombre and slower version.

## CHANGE OF THE GUARD

THE PENULTIMATE song on *Can't Buy a Thrill* provided Baxter with an opportunity to solo... and what a solo. Everything about the song is upbeat; Jim Hodder obviously enjoyed having the freedom for a good thrash; Becker's bass nudges in and out like an inquisitive cat and all join in together for a good na-na-na sing-a-long. "Skunk" then enters to dismantle all the good work (shredding the whole shebang with his axe).

## TURN THAT HEARTBEAT OVER AGAIN

CERTAINLY one of the more sophisticated and abstruse numbers on the album, both lyrically and musically 'Turn That Heartbeat Over Again' was one of the tunes that would embarrass Denny Dias years later. "We just weren't up to it," he said. To the average Steely Dan fan it certainly wasn't that bad; workman-like drums from Hodder, a competent guitar solo, simple bass line and tinkling bells at the fade.

# Countdown To Ecstasy

Probe SPB 1079, July 1973; current LP MCA MCL (1982),
also FAME FA 3069 (1983) CD: MCAD 37041 (1985)

**S**TEELY **D**AN'S SECOND ALBUM WAS RELEASED IN JULY 1973. RECORDED DURING the week with weekends reserved for gigging this prolonged and heavy schedule proved difficult for the band, especially Becker and Fagen who were trying to write enough material for the follow up to *Can't Buy A Thrill*. They had been advised by their record company to appoint Joel Cohen from Kudo III (who'd once managed Three Dog Night) as their manager, and once the band took off Cohen saw a golden opportunity to make money for Steely Dan and himself. Unfortunately Becker and Fagen didn't share his enthusiasm; they were much more interested in the artistic and creative side of things, and gradually their resistance gained the upper hand.

Becker and Fagen weren't unduly concerned with pressures of trying to match the two hit singles from *Thrill*. Instead, they luxuriated in the relative freedom granted in the studio – freedom which enabled them to be far more meticulous than on the debut. As things turned out, they were unable to capitalise on their initial singles success, releasing the wrong songs at the wrong time. This consequent lack of hits meant that the album didn't sell as well either, failing to crack the Top 30.

The almost surreal cover painting was a watercolour by Donald Fagen's then girlfriend Dorothy White, known as 'Dotty of Hollywood'. When ABC boss Jay Lasker saw the proposed cover, he objected on the grounds that it featured only three naked aliens, while there were five members in the band. Dotty argued that it wasn't a depiction of the group itself, but Lasker insisted and so she went back and incorporated a further two standing figures behind those seated without altering the impact of the painting. The disembodied hand on the board in the band photograph on the rear cover belonged to Roger Nichols.

Unfortunately for David Palmer, Becker and Fagen had by now come to realise that his voice was not the sound they sought for Steely Dan, and he was relegated to a couple of background vocal appearances on *Countdown To Ecstasy*. Palmer left the band by (almost) mutual consent before the album was finished, and would be replaced by Royce Jones, from a band called Odyssey. He was recruited for live gigs (his only appearance on a Steely Dan album being *Countdown To Ecstasy*.)

Meanwhile Steely Dan augmented their touring band by hiring two sexy background singers named Gloria Granola and Jenny Soule, who became known as 'Porky And Bucky'. The girls were brought in to enhance the visual appeal of Steely Dan as much as anything, since one brutally honest reviewer had already described them as "the ugliest band in the world". This pleased Becker and Fagen in a perverse way, because they were totally opposed to the idea of smoke bombs, face masks and other image-orientated buffoonery of the time. Once they had Porky and Bucky in the live band, if they were in the right mood, Steely Dan would come out and perform The Angels' 1963 hit, 'My Boyfriend's Back' as an encore.

Jeff Baxter told one interviewer that it had been Becker and Fagen's intention to write a song about a marine and his quest to "get laid" (which would perhaps fit with the album title), but they were slightly worried about getting into trouble with the State Department, and so abandoned the idea.

Donald Fagen was still uneasy about doing all of the singing on stage, and if they'd been able to find a suitable candidate, he would have surrendered the studio leads too. One singer who they thought might work well with their material was Scottish singer, Gerry Rafferty from Stealers Wheel, and another was Elliott Lurie from Looking Glass, who had had a US number 1 hit with 'Brandy (You're A Fine Girl)'.

In England, Probe adopted an aggressive publicity campaign for the album, running a series of ads on Radio Luxembourg, taking full-page ads in the music press and distributing display cards to retailers. Curiously, Probe also sponsored a Steely Dan balloon race at a Radio Luxembourg motor race meeting at Brands Hatch in Kent. Early Probe pressings of the album in the UK had the benefit of a full lyric sheet, complete with cryptic comments about each song (again rendered by Becker and Fagen themselves).

---

## BODHISATTVA

THE OPENING song on *Countdown To Ecstasy* was written primarily by Donald Fagen. It cast a humorous look at the then fashion for Eastern religion, with many middle-class Americans pursuing the teachings of various forms of Buddhism, and the majority of them failing to achieve any kind of enlightenment. This stunning rocker was ideal as an opener at Steely Dan gigs. However, unlike a lot of their other material, it has been a little overused in recent years, has not worn quite as well, and, 20 years on, lacks the impact which it had when Steely Dan were a "real and hungry band".

---

## RAZOR BOY

AFTER the raucous heat of 'Bodhisattva', 'Razor Boy' cools things down somewhat. Victor Feldman plays the vibes and the great Ray Brown plays string bass on this song, yet another with an enigmatic lyric which sounds like it's possibly based on a dream. On the lyric sheet Becker and Fagen refer to the "'Giant Girlfriend of the Camden, New Jersey Area' who sees the spectre of Benny King as a child in a nightmare of cosmic proportions." It's Jeff Baxter's all-time favourite Steely Dan song.

## THE BOSTON RAG

LONG after the release of the record, Walter Becker said, "I always think the nice thing about 'The Boston Rag' was that it took place in New York." With the chorus written by Donald Fagen and the verses by Walter Becker, it centres around an old band mate of Donald Fagen's named Lonnie Yongue who, in his own words, "used to black out every night." With a cracking intro, a really powerful chorus and Fagen singing cooly and effortlessly over Ben Benay's crisp acoustic guitar, 'The Boston Rag' climaxes with Jeff Baxter's guitar solo, which he says was inspired by Bach's 'Toccata and Fugue', which he'd just taught himself to play.

## YOUR GOLD TEETH

WHILE Steely Dan were in the middle of recording *Countdown To Ecstasy*, David Palmer came back from the dentist one day with a bridge fitted. After subjecting him to the occasional cruel joke, Donald Fagen went out into the studio, sat at the piano and proceeded to play a song with the lyrics "Do you throw out your gold teeth?" It freaked out David Palmer, and from that moment on, the rest of the band became more and more paranoid about being fired themselves. In Palmer's case, the axe was already on its way down.

As impenetrable today as it was back in '73, 'Your Gold Teeth' name checks Cathy Berberian (an avant garde screamer and shouter), borrows a lyric from Count Basie and Joe Williams' 'Going to Chicago Blues' ("There ain't nothing in Chicago for a monkey woman to do") and features a dazzling guitar solo from Denny Dias.

## SHOW BIZ KIDS

'SHOW Biz Kids' was one of those songs on which Becker and Fagen could not get the perfectly steady drum track which they wanted, and since there were no drum machines in those days, Roger Nichols came up with the idea of making a 24-track, 8-bar tape loop which involved a lot of tape. They trailed it out through the door into the studio, around a little idler which was set up on a camera tripod, back into the studio and copied it to a second 24 track machine.

At this point ABC were letting Steely Dan choose their own singles, although the band were not renowned for their understanding of the commercial market. Their choice of 'Show Biz Kids' was a case in point: it went absolutely nowhere in the charts, despite having been edited down to a more radio-friendly length. This editing enabled the record company to cut out the expletive "fuck". (Welsh band, Super Furry Animals finally got Fagen's permission to sample this line for their single 'The Man Don't Give A Fuck,' in which the word is used 55 times). Steely Dan did show some concern over the use of the 'F' word, but though they tried, nothing else fitted and they decided to stick with their original choice. "We're sadder but wiser in relation to that. It's always comforting to know that you've got something potentially obscene on AM radio'. Becker said.

Rick Derringer's slide guitar break was recorded at Carabou Ranch in Colorado. As the song heads towards the fade, it descends into chaos with all manner of shouts buried in the mix. Two of these were actually credited on the sleeve: Steely Dan's Tour Manager Warren Wallace ("Grunt") gruffly asks "Is this the band that's looking for a lead singer?" and then John Famular does his expert impersonation of an airline pilot clicking on the microphone to announce "This is your captain speaking." Becker and Fagen had lived in Los Angeles for a few years by this time, and were obviously not impressed with the quality of life in California, nor its inhabitants' integrity. 'Show Biz Kids' put LA very firmly in its place.

Radio One DJ John Peel reviewed the single in *Sounds* and liked Derringer's slide playing, and what he saw as Becker and Fagen's healthy cynicism. He also lamented the omission of the rude word which he said "might have prodded the more impressionable among you into raging uncontrolled copulation in the high street."

A frequently asked question of Becker and Fagen for years afterwards concerned the nature of the background chant which, in fact, is "You go to Lost Wages."

## MY OLD SCHOOL

BECKER and Fagen already had the arrangement for 'My Old School' when they went in to record the track, since they had already played it numerous times in concert. Set at Bard College in upstate New York where Becker and Fagen met in 1967, the song was part fact, part fiction, the latter being an imaginary college romance problem.

"Skunk" Baxter was an absolute guitar freak, making and customising his own instruments, and the blinding solo on 'My Old School' was played on a Fender Stratocaster which he'd just finished working on in the parking lot at Valley Sound. When asked what he remembers about recording 'My Old School,' producer Gary Katz' only comment was: "Jeffery turning red playing the solo."

The song still has a special place in countless Steely Dan fans' hearts, and during the 1996 world tour, when it appeared in the encores the response was rapturous. 'My Old School' was the second single from *Countdown To Ecstasy* in October, 1973, but it fared no better than 'Show Biz Kids' and Steely Dan had totally bombed on the singles front.

## PEARL OF THE QUARTER

THIS was the B side of the 'My Old School' single, and seems to be about a beautiful but vulnerable girl who has forsaken her sweetheart for a perilously sleazy life as a street girl. The story has a happy ending when a 'not entirely by chance' encounter results in a reconciliation.

'Pearl of the Quarter' was written before *Can't Buy A Thrill* came out but did not fit into Becker and Fagen's (then) scheme of things. In the very early days Steely Dan used to perform it live, but bootlegs containing the song are extremely rare, if not non-existent.

## KING OF THE WORLD

BOTH Becker and Fagen had been sci-fi fans as kids, and Walter Becker stated that 'King Of The World' had been written after watching the 1962 Ray Milland film *Panic In The Year Zero*. The film told the story of a family on a fishing trip in the mountains outside Los Angeles who are hit by a nuclear attack. Becker and Fagen's composition examines the Armageddon situation and the pointlessness of any kind of existence after such an attack.

Becker laid on the floor of the studio and whined "I think my face is on fire." Once again, Jeff Baxter played the solo using an Echoplex (he was not a great lover of effects pedals). One night during the mixing of 'King Of The World', only Denny Dias and Roger Nicholas were left working – Becker and Fagen having long since gone home, and Gary Katz having fallen asleep on the studio floor. Dias came up with a technique of playing a verse, then a chorus and splicing the two-track tape together. This made it possible to do things that no musician could perform in real time. Nichols said the mix sounded like sonic wallpaper – it sounded so perfect that afterwards you couldn't remember hearing it. Nichols and Dias were still in the studio at 10 am the next morning when the next band booked in came knocking for the start of their session. Dias never stayed up all night to mix again. Becker and Fagen rewarded him for his efforts with a credit as "Stereo Mixmaster".

# Pretzel Logic

Probe SPBA 6282, March 1974, reissued as ABC ABCL 5045,
October 1974; current LP MCA MCL 1781 (1984), CD MCAD 37042 (1986)

**B**Y THE TIME STEELY DAN BEGAN RECORDING THEIR THIRD ALBUM, CRACKS that had been appearing in the personnel had widened into chasms, and although the five piece band was pictured on the LP's inner sleeve, Jim Hodder didn't play on the record at all (he was relegated to singing background vocals on 'Parker's Band'). Much as Hodder was miffed by his exile, Becker and Fagen had promised him "terms" whereby he would still receive financial compensation. Most of the drumming on *Pretzel Logic* fell to Jim Gordon, once of Derek & The Dominos, who would later be sentenced to life imprisonment for the murder of his mother.

By the time *Pretzel Logic* was recorded, Gary Katz had steered Becker and Fagen into the workshop situation, so the cream of Los Angeles' session population were also drafted in: Chuck Rainey on bass, Michael Omartian – piano, and Deane Parks – guitar. Victor Feldman was already in the fold.

After *Can't Buy A Thrill* and *Countdown To Ecstasy*, Becker and Fagen wanted to complete the trilogy with another bawdy title, but failed to come up with anything suitable. Having spent much of their time touring, they had also struggled somewhat in the songwriting department, and were forced to delve back into their old songbook to complete the album. They resurrected three songs: 'Barrytown', 'Parker's Band', and 'Charlie Freak' from their time with Kenny Vance.

Hodder and Baxter had formed a team to combat and oppose Becker and Fagen at every opportunity. They wanted to be out on the road partying, getting laid and doing all the things that touring rock and roll bands are supposed to do. Denny Dias was caught between the two factions, but was unwilling to do anything that might displease Becker and Fagen.

With hi-fi nut Roger Nichols on board, Becker was also eager to try out the latest studio equipment. For *Pretzel Logic*, Steely Dan installed a pair of 5 foot speakers in Village Recorders called Magnaplaners, although not everyone held them in as high a regard – Michael Omartian said they were paper thin and sounded "just goofy".

Steely Dan included their first (and last) cover version on *Pretzel Logic*, a rendition of Duke Ellington and Bubber Miley's 'East St. Louis Toodle-Oo'. Fagen sent the Duke a copy of the album for his 75th birthday, but he died within a month of that date, so Fagen never found out whether he got to hear it or not. As usual, the album had an interesting sleeve. Fagen and

Gary Katz thought it might be amusing to use a photograph of a pretzel vendor in Central Park. At the time the weather in New York was freezing, and they didn't really want snow in shot, but time was tight and they couldn't wait. The pretzel seller refused to sign a release form for the rights to use his photograph, but after some investigation, ABC discovered he didn't have the necessary licence and so used the photo anyway.

A short album (34 minutes) of short songs, *Pretzel Logic* was released in March 1974. Two months later, Steely Dan arrived in England for a tour, but it was curtailed after only five dates when Fagen was taken ill. Although they only played five shows, the band's consensus of opinion was that they were among the best gigs they'd ever performed – with Manchester's Palace Theatre being the absolute standout – so the cancelling of the second half of the tour was a cruel twist of fate. Steely Dan also loved the English audiences who listened attentively all the time they were playing and only applauded (or bawled at them) between songs.

## RIKKI DON'T LOSE THAT NUMBER

ONE OF Steely Dan's greatest singles and the opening song on *Pretzel Logic*, 'Rikki Don't Lose That Number' is another song which critics thought was wrapped up in code. The song had nothing to do with Rick Derringer (a very common misconception and one which he continues to promote), and nothing to do with a marijuana cigarette; the choice of name was simply due to the presence of a stunning girl who Becker and Fagen knew when they were at Bard.

It re-established Steely Dan in the top ten again (number four in the *Billboard* charts), but didn't chart in the UK until 1979, and then only reached number 58. It was nominated for best pop vocal in the Grammies.

Becker and Fagen had borrowed the intro from Horace Silver's jazz composition, 'Song To My Father', although Donald Fagen explained that it was simply a Brazilian bass line, and when Jim Gordon saw the chart he automatically started playing that beat. It was the last song to be mixed, and they were hopeful that if it came out as well as anticipated it would make a good opener.

Jeff Baxter's guitar was again plugged straight into the board. His solo is incredible – the notes blending together, tumbling from his fingers with the deftness and speed of a magician casting coins into thin air. The song was covered by Tom Robinson, who had a minor hit with it (coincidentally Number 58, exactly the same as Steely Dan but five years later). The *Citizen Steely Dan* box bet version edited out the 25 second flopanda intro.

## NIGHT BY NIGHT

'NIGHT By Night' was recorded in the barn at Cherokee Sound in Chatsworth, and Becker and Fagen admitted on one occasion that it had been written purely for commercial purposes. Jim Hodder was unable to give Becker and Fagen what they wanted from the drum track, so in the middle of the night, Denny Dias came up with the idea of using Jeff Porcaro, a very gifted 19-year-old drummer who would join the touring band and become a Steely Dan stalwart. The barn had a rope and noose hanging from the rafters and when Porcaro saw this, he joked "I know you guys have a rough reputation on musicians, but this is ridiculous." His performance here simply towers above the rest of the musicians, with all its youthful impetuosity.

Porcaro turned up with keyboard player David Paich and the song, with its staccato horns and bleating guitars, seemed to sum up Porcaro's happy go lucky philosophy on life to a tee. Live for today and let tomorrow take care of itself. Whenever Becker and Fagen needed a hole in a song filling, they'd call in Jeff Baxter and grind the solo out of him.

## ANY MAJOR DUDE WILL TELL YOU

ALMOST a forgotten Steely Dan tune, but a stunning and emo-tional three minute pop song, Jim Gordon's snare snaps at your eardrum like a trap on a rabbit's leg. It was nailed in the second take, and was over almost before the band knew they were recording it. The guitar part was divided into two sections – one which needed no vibrato and one which absolutely did require the use of vibrato. To get around this problem, Denny Dias (who did not bend strings in his playing) played the first part, then handed the guitar to Jeff Baxter who completed his part. Roger Nichols then punched it into the tape machine.

Becker and Fagen betrayed their literary leanings with a line about a squonk; a mythical woods animal that has the ability to cry itself into a bag of tears, and which had most of the session players shrugging their shoulders and furtively enquiring as to its meaning.

## BARRYTOWN

BARRYTOWN is a hamlet near Bard College of which Becker and Fagen had plenty of first hand experience, and they used this song to denigrate the small town mentality – the so-called town and gown conflict. This version is much fatter than their original demo. Fagen's voice has more conviction on the track, in fact he wrote it without any input from his partner. "I don't know if it came off so great anyway," Fagen said, but he was being his usual overly critical self.

Michael Omartian's joyous piano introduction belies the undercurrent contained in the lyrics, which incredibly were exactly the same as their sparse piano and vocal demo. Dan fan William Gibson named a settlement after it in his novel *Count Zero*.

## EAST ST. LOUIS TOODLE-OO

THIS song was originally recorded in 1925 by Duke Ellington. Becker and Fagen went out and obtained all available versions of the song, each one slightly different in detail and arrangement, and combined all of them for their own version. They thought it amusing that a wah-wah guitar sounded just like a muted trumpet had some 50 years before, but that a complicated set of electronics was needed in order to replicate the sound.

Fagen himself played the piano solo which Becker explained was "a composite of four bad clarinet solos" from the original. Becker played Tricky Sam Nanton's trombone solo on a pedal-steel guitar through a Fuzztone (as well as bass), his first appearance on guitar on a Steely Dan record.

For several years it was Annie Nightingale's theme tune on her Radio 1 Sunday evening request show.

## PARKER'S BAND

BECKER and Fagen's tribute to Charlie Parker was already about six years old when they recorded it as Steely Dan. Featuring the double drums of Jeff Porcaro and Jim Gordon, and another fine Denny Dias solo, 'Parker's Band' is a pacey, stylish paean to one of their favourite jazz heroes, and includes a quote from 'Bongo Bop', and references to other Parker compositions, 'Relaxing at Camarillo' and 'Groovin' High'. The former was inspired by a period of recuperation at a hospital in California.

Just listen to the way Denny Dias' guitar takes you into that alliterative first line: "Savoy Sides presents a new saxophone sensation." Becker and Jim Hodder assist Fagen on vocals, then in comes alto sax player Plas Johnson to play the saxes at the end.

## THROUGH WITH BUZZ

PERHAPS the only time "filler" ever to find its way onto a Steely Dan album. 'Through With Buzz' is one and a half minutes of strings, and a virtually non-existent lyric about a friend of very dubious merit. Even the punch line in the last verse, "maybe he's a fairy", fails to save it.

## PRETZEL LOGIC

THE TITLE song, according to Donald Fagen, was allegedly about time travel – hence the line "I have never met Napoleon/but I plan to find the time." Becker and Fagen envisaged the "platform" as a teleportation device.

This bluesy, funky song induced Walter Becker to play the solo in a laid back and almost matter of fact manner, but it fits perfectly; Jim Gordon executes a slow shuffle, and Fagen's voice dominates the whole rhythm section.

This was another live favourite, especially once they had hired Michael McDonald to assist Fagen with key lines.

## WITH A GUN

A GALLOPING depiction of a business relationship gone bad describing a man who has absolutely no qualms about settling his debts by taking out the creditor in question with a Luger. Acoustic guitars provide a rhythmic intro before Jim Gordon's drum kicks in to propel the song forward at break-neck speed.

## CHARLIE FREAK

SET AMONG the other tales of violence, time travel and deception, 'Charlie Freak' is about as emotional as Becker and Fagen ever get. The vagrant of the title is hungry and cold, lonely and bored, so he sells his last worthwhile possession – a gold ring – to a friend only to spend the money he earns from this deal on his chosen drug, and winds up in the city morgue. After identifying the body, the buyer returns the ring to Charlie's finger which helps to absolve his guilt.

The cello parts were achieved by channelling Baxter's pedal steel guitar through a Fuzztone.

## MONKEY IN YOUR SOUL

THE ALBUM closes with the growling backdrop and funky saxes of 'Monkey In Your Soul,' a cruelly underrated and overlooked song.

# Katy Lied

ABC ABCL 5094, April 1975; current LP MCA MCL 1800 (1984),
CD MCAD 37043 (1986)

**R**ELEASED IN APRIL 1975, *KATY LIED* FOUND STEELY DAN CONTINUING WITH the short pop song format, but although only one song, 'Your Gold Teeth II', lasted in excess of four minutes, the brevity of the tracks didn't detract from the beauty of the material. Becker and Fagen had asked Michael Omartian to go out and buy a new piano. He went to David Abell Music across the street from the studio, and bought a Bosendorfer which was delivered to the studio that same afternoon and became the focal instrument of the whole album.

With no concerts or travelling to trouble them now, Becker and Fagen were able to retreat into the ABC recording studio in North Hollywood to work on *Katy Lied* without interruption. As with *Countdown To Ecstasy*, Donald Fagen's girlfriend Dorothy White provided the album cover – this time a blurred close up photograph of a grasshopper like insect called a Katydid. They liked the play on words it evoked. The rear cover was based on a design of Fifties jazz label Atlantic which Becker and Fagen much admired.

When doing interviews, Becker and Fagen spouted about their intention to write songs about Da Nang, Gerald Ford, the Kennedy assassination and even the Congress of Vienna, which dealt with the disposition of Napoleon's empire in 1814/15. Although these particular grandiose subjects never appeared, topics which weren't by any means your standard pop fare were covered: a stock market crash, a visit to a fascist rally and the corruption of teenagers by porno movies.

After using Jeff Porcaro on their *Pretzel Logic* tour, Becker and Fagen employed him almost exclusively on the *Katy Lied* sessions (he played on every track except 'Any World That I'm Welcome To', which featured Hal Blaine). Michael McDonald was also co-opted from the tour, because of his tremendous blend with Donald Fagen, and lent his very distinctive textures to background vocals.

Once recording was finished, Steely Dan decided to use a DBX sound reduction system for mixing. This proved to be a disastrous decision, because when all the mixes were played back, the DBX system had damaged the sound quality on the tape. Despite long and heroic efforts, including a visit to the DBX factory in Boston, and the special manufacture by the company of a machine with external controls to manipulate the internal mechanics, they were never able to fully recover the original sound. Gary Katz was absolutely devastated, and said at the time that the album came within a whisker of being scrapped completely. Becker and Fagen soon got over it, and wrote some tongue-in-cheek sleeve notes about some of the hardware they had used to make the album, including German microphones and a 24-channel tape recorder. No mention was made of the DBX system, though Becker put it very succinctly later: "Machines ten, Humans nil".

## BLACK FRIDAY

THE TERM 'Black Friday' has often been used in the US and UK to describe a day of financial crisis, and the opening song on the album detailed such a stock market crash. Donald Fagen said that "it was really about the original 1929 crash" but, oddly enough, several market crashes happened not long after it was written. ABC took it as the first single, backed by 'Throw Back The Little Ones', which could only reach number 37.

In Becker and Fagen's song, the crooked speculator, now that his scam has been exposed, absconds to Australia with his ill-gotten gains "with nothing to do but feed all the kangaroos." Of all the places they could choose for their protagonist to seek refuge, Muswell Brook in deepest New South Wales leapt at them from their world atlas.

David Paich and Michael Omartian duel away on electric piano and piano respectively, Walter Becker commits his most rollicking solo to tape and, altogether, the result is as thoroughly out-and-out rock as *Katy Lied* ever gets.

## BAD SNEAKERS

BELATEDLY, Gary Katz and Becker and Fagen realised that 'Bad Sneakers' should have been the lead-off single off the album. In fact, they made it the second single in August 1975, with 'Chain Lightning' as its B-side, but it was a futile gesture and the single went nowhere.

Sporting another divine Becker and Fagen melody 'Bad Sneakers' could be about their unease with the LA lifestyle, and in the first four lines they are looking back at the original Steely Dan line up, and perhaps how things should have been. They are dreaming of going home to New York, as even the vastly improved climate cannot compensate for California's lack of artistic vitality.

Hugh McCracken locks the song into a great groove with his rhythm guitar, and Becker's guitar solo – although he allegedly took an hour to execute each bar – is sheer perfection, an orgasm in an instant.

## ROSE DARLING

DONALD Fagen was an avid reader of Vladimir Nabokov, the writer whose controversial 1961 novel *Lolita* provided them with the title for a song about an illicit affair, illicit drugs and murderous intentions.

Jeff Porcaro's snare drum is crisp, Fagen's phrasing uses a lot of cadences like Bob Dylan, and Michael McDonald's vocals are stacked up behind Fagen like so many 19th century buffalo hides on the high plains. Dean Parks played the guitar solo which was written out for him – a most unusual occurrence since the whole point of hiring crack session players was to utilise their input and expression on a solo.

## DADDY DON'T LIVE IN THAT NEW YORK CITY NO MORE

"NOO YAWK, just like I pictured it," as it said in Stevie Wonder's 'Living In The City'. Downtown Manhattan provides the setting for Becker and Fagen's very own film noir. The 'Daddy' in the title is a gangster driven out of the city by threats. His former fine lifestyle has been replaced by one not nearly so attractive.

This song was the first time that Becker and Fagen had used Larry Carlton on an album; he played rhythm guitar, but was soon elevated to a much more prominent position in the band when they realised the depth of his talent.

## DOCTOR WU

THIS was the first song written after the *Pretzel Logic* tour wound up. Gary Katz later admitted that the song was emotionally crushing to him, and that it was one of his three favourite Steely Dan songs. Phil Woods, jazz saxophonist, stepped in to play the alto solo, and Donald Fagen was so astounded by his superlative first take performance that he asked him to play it again, just so he could hear it.

Fagen explained that the song was about a "kind of love dope triangle" where one of the partners comes under the influence of someone or something else, and is seduced by the dealer who provides them with their drug.

Jeff Porcaro tried to emulate John Guerin's drumming on Joni Mitchell's *Court And Spark* and that new Bosendorfer piano is rich, warm and flawlessly played by Michael Omartian. Four minutes in an aural paradise.

## EVERYONE'S GONE TO THE MOVIES

'EVERYONE'S Gone To The Movies' opened side two and had originally been written even before Steely Dan existed. Copyrighted in 1971, the demo version eventually appeared on the *Citizen Steely Dan* box set in 1993. This 1975 version still features Victor Feldman on percussion, who is the only musician to have appeared on all seven Steely Dan studio albums, save for Becker and Fagen themselves.

This was another song freshly retrieved from the vaults for Steely Dan's 1996 tour, and Becker and Fagen shared the vocals between them.

## YOUR GOLD TEETH II

A N INTRICATE and difficult tune with tricky time signatures, 'Your Gold Teeth II' initially proved hard to get in the studio. Using a rhythm section of Porcaro, bassist Chuck Rainey and keyboardist Michael Omartian, they kept trying it without success, until Fagen gave Porcaro a Charles Mingus record to listen to overnight with Dannie Richmond on drums. He studied it closely and next day they succeeded in pleasing Becker and Fagen with a take. Porcaro later described it as "pure bebop".

It was basically a sequel to Countdown To Ecstasy's 'Your Gold Teeth', and stemmed from a jam which had developed on extended live versions of 'Do It Again.' However, the Katy Lied version was closer to the original song which was never recorded. "It was," Walter Becker said, "just a simple sort of waltz."

On a Canadian bootleg of Katy Lied out takes, which includes studio chatter, Fagen can be heard

reacting to Denny Dias' stupendous guitar solo with the words, "Holy fuck, that's great!" In a nutshell.

## CHAIN LIGHTNING

A SHORT, slow, blues inspired song about a visit to a fascist rally, summed up in only 71 words, less than three minutes, and one which was the source of much fun for Becker and Fagen during interviews. "No-one will ever come close to [unravelling] that one," they proudly claimed. Fagen said that he was going to say "Forty years later" before the second verse, but decided that it wasn't a good musical idea. On the above mentioned bootleg, Fagen can be heard actually trying this. Becker was pleased that Rick Derringer had to re-think his approach to the solo in coming up with something a little different due to the constantly modulating chords. The song later became a staple of the New York Rock and Soul Revue shows in the Nineties.

## ANY WORLD THAT I'M WELCOME TO

F EATURING the legendary Hal Blaine on drums, this was yet another resurrected number from Becker and Fagen's old exercise book of songs. They had recorded it in New York with Kenny Vance, had offered it to Linda Hoover, and also later to Dusty Springfield (with whom they'd worked on a Thomas

Jefferson Kaye record). As neither of those versions ever saw the light of day, they figured they might as well record it themselves. Michael McDonald lends his voice to proceedings in the chorus, and lifts it to otherwise unattainable heights.

## THROW BACK THE LITTLE ONES

THE MAIN redeeming feature to 'Throw Back The Little Ones' is another Elliot Randall guitar solo. Lyrically, this seems fairly meaningless, but one suspects that the words cannot be as straightforward as they seem. The superimposed triads at the end were Michael Omartian's idea. A low key end to the album.

# The Royal Scam

ABC ABCL 5161, May 1976; Current LP MCA MCL 1708 (1982),
CD MCAD 37044 (1986)

*THE ROYAL SCAM* SAW THE INTRODUCTION OF BERNARD "PRETTY" PURDIE into Steely Dan's ever expanding catalogue of session players, and thenceforth he became a Steely Dan regular. Purdie played on all the tunes except 'Don't Take Me Alive,' which featured Rick Marotta. The most telling use was made of Larry Carlton, whose guitar work and solos define the whole album.

As the use of studio players increased, so Becker and Fagen's own playing roles diminished accordingly. At one point Fagen even admitted that it wouldn't bother him if he didn't play on his own album. Meanwhile, they started recording each tune with six or seven different rhythm sections, switching players in and out so often that seemingly, no-one knew what was going on. Endless experimentation became the name of the game.

The album came out simultaneously on both sides of the Atlantic in May 1976, but in the meantime Becker and Fagen had been receiving mailed threats from ABC concerning protracted recording schedules. These would continue even while they were making *Aja*, despite the fact that each album had sold more than the last.

Becker and Fagen came to Europe to promote the album, and during interviews once again made a stream of bold statements. These included such gems as "We were trying to capture the inflection of The King James Bible (107th psalm)." Ostensibly, they were looking at studios with a view to recording in Europe. Fagen's fascination with the Little Corporal drew him to the Napoleonic Museum in Monaco, while Becker and Roger Nichols attended the Monaco Grand Prix because the latter was an acclaimed motor racing photographer as well as studio engineer.

Steely Dan began recording *The Royal Scam* in LA's Davlin Studios in 1975 with Elliott Scheiner engineering. After two weeks, and with nothing in the can, they abandoned Davlin and headed back to New York to try their luck at Scheiner's home studio, A&R. Having previously contented themselves with 24 track recording, Becker and Fagen were persuaded by Scheiner to experiment with linking up two 16-track machines to give 32 tracks. Like kids with new toys, and with a fresh sense of purpose, they booked a succession of New York musicians. The sessions proved dynamic and soon, half the album's tracks were on tape. Unfortunately, when Scheiner came to edit the tapes he found that he wasn't able to do so because something hadn't been fully explained to him beforehand.

Consequently all that work went down the drain.

Steely Dan went back to Los Angeles and transferred all the material back to 24-track, dismissed Scheiner and hired Roger Nichols and Barney Perkins to mix the album. Compared to previous records, *The Royal Scam* presented a much bigger bass and drum sound. It was more live sounding, and considering the majority of the subject matter, was edgy and provocative.

Another superb cover showed a man asleep on a Boston bus station bench as sky scrapers and angry skies towered above him. Each building had a different animal's snarling head superimposed onto it. At the centre of the cover was a king cobra about to strike at a mongoose on its neighbouring edifice. The skyscrapers had been painted by Zox for a Van Morrison album cover. When Morrison abandoned his project, photographer Charlie Ganse and Ed Caraeff came up with the idea of using Ganse's photo of the vagrant with the Zox painting. They took the photo to a Hollywood specialist who touched it up and succeeded in matching the tone of the painting.

---

## KID CHARLEMAGNE

THE OPENING song on the album was basically a first night take at A & R in New York, with a band consisting of Bernard Purdie on drums, Chuck Rainey – bass, Don Grolnick – keyboards, Larry Carlton – guitar and the omnipresent Victor Feldman. It's the story of a casualty of the Sixties – "A chemist, a chef, an artist, a maker," as Becker and Fagen variously described him – who, at the turn of the decade, found himself redundant, alone and on the most wanted list. In his heyday, he'd had everything, but was so wrapped up in the trappings of success that he failed to anticipate that it wouldn't last forever.

Becker and Fagen denied that Timothy Leary or Charles Manson was the basis for the character in the song, although Becker did at one point state that their fictitious Kid was based on a real individual "who hung over the song like the sword of Damocles," but refused to name him. In a separate interview, Becker mentioned the Grateful Dead associate Augustus Stanley Owsley as another possible model for the character.

'Kid Charlemagne' was released as a single in the US, backed with 'Green Earrings', and although it was unquestionably the stand-out song on the album, it only reached number 82.

Purdie's sibilant hi-hat acts as punctuation in the song, while Rainey's bass is suitably fractious. Fagen never sang higher than the line "is there gas in the car?" and Carlton's guitar solos, overdubbed later, will surely never be surpassed.

## THE CAVES OF ALTAMIRA

BECKER and Fagen were still not averse to resorting back to their old book of songs when the need arose. 'The Caves of Altamira' had originally been demoed (in a much more rhythmically complex version) with Kenny Vance. The caves themselves are an archaeologist's dream – a song based on the cave paintings of deer, bison, wild cattle and goats to be found west of Santander in Spain. A young boy, a loner, finds escapism by sneaking out in the dead of night to visit his own little world, and being transported back in time by the images before him. This time around Becker and Fagen omitted the third verse of the song.

## DON'T TAKE ME ALIVE

'DON'T Take Me Alive' reflects Becker and Fagen's wish to concentrate on more topical material on the album. After a run of news items in Los Angeles about armed sieges and wild public shoot-outs, they decided to write a song exposing the fact that "Terrorism had become a way of life" for some people, describing the individual madness associated with its proponents.

Fagen takes the role of the robotic psychopath holed up in his apartment with explosives and numerous weapons and with a determination to spin out the con-frontation for as long as possible before his inevitable demise. Becker and Fagen's instruction to Larry Carlton was to turn his amp up as loud as possible for the malevolent introduction.

## SIGN IN STRANGER

FOLLOWING the earthly gunfire and violence of 'Don't Take Me Alive', comes the other worldliness of 'Sign In Stranger,' a sci-fi short story set on a distant planet which is a haven for criminals and murderers, extortionists and rapists, where all one's previous wrong-doings can be erased quite easily.

Paul Griffin improvised a suitable interplanetary piano solo and Elliot Randall whipped off another guitar solo.

## THE FEZ

AN EXAMPLE of Becker and Fagen's sense of humour 'The Fez' was at this point the only Steely Dan song ever to share a writing credit with someone other than themselves. As the song was built up in the studio and featured a melody suggested by Paul Griffin which became extremely prominent, Becker and Fagen thought it wise to allow Griffin a songwriting credit. They also joked about the similarity of this melody to a piece of classical music. By giving Griffin a co-credit, they ensured that he would take the brunt of the impact should a plagiarism case ever come to court.

Written long before the advent of AIDS, 'The Fez' is not about the use of synthetic protection, but more likely about a fetish for making love wearing unusual head gear. Fagen described it as a "disco song which suddenly has a lot of chords", and said that "you can dance to parts of it, it's just that you have to stop in the middle once in a while." But Becker and Fagen were too clever by half because very few people got the joke – either lyrically or musically.

The track was released as a single, but stalled at number 59 in the US.

## GREEN EARRINGS

YET ANOTHER minimalist lyric from Becker and Fagen tells a sketchy tale about a jewel thief, but the track is more memorable for Denny Dias' early guitar solo, Elliott Randall's more note-heavy second solo, and Bernard Purdie's machine gun snare drum sound.

## HAITIAN DIVORCE

WHILE working with Becker and Fagen, Scheiner had told them how his lawyer had advised him to go to Haiti in order to get a quickie divorce through in a couple of months for tax purposes. Sensing a good story, they astounded Scheiner when they eventually brought this song in to record based

around his own experiences. (They had, of course, added a few amusing twists to the story for the sake of interest). In interviews, Becker and Fagen enveloped the song in more cryptic comments than any of their other creations. "It's a fierce and terrible ritual," Fagen said. "You wouldn't want your sister to go through it." But the most cryptic statement was told to Richard Cromelin in *New Musical Express* when they specifically asked him to write: "Donald and Walter are well aware of the fact that Aida is not joking with you."

It became Steely Dan's biggest UK hit, reaching number 17 in December 1976, but didn't come out as a single in the US. Dean Parks played the guitar lines, and Becker memorised Parks' solo from a quick mix, took it home and, using a voice box, distorted the notes into their guttural state. Reggae hadn't been all that popular in America up to this point, and Becker and Fagen decided it would be interesting and, no doubt, amusing to compose a reggae song with a lot of jazz chords.

## EVERYTHING YOU DID

BECAUSE Steely Dan were often lumped together with The Eagles as being representative of West Coast rock, Becker and Fagen developed a running joke about how The Eagles were their only competition. This surfaced in the lyric of 'Everything You Did', in the couplet "turn up The Eagles/the neighbours are listening" which was erroneously regarded by Don Henley and Glenn Frey as a compliment. (They would 'return the compliment' in 'Hotel California' by using the line "they stab it with their steely knives.")

The narrator of this song is a glutton for punishment – he knows his lover has committed sexual indiscretions and wants to know every last gory detail.

## THE ROYAL SCAM

THE TITLE song of the album, some six minutes long, was an ambitious tale about Puerto Rican immigrants coming to the US to seek a better life. Once again, Becker and Fagen toyed with interviewers, sometimes denying that this interpretation was correct, at others admitting that "because the interpretation is so accurate, I wouldn't even want to comment further."

'The Royal Scam' featured a fine vocal from Fagen, set against an eerie trumpet, swelling brass and a menacing organ. Fagen told Richard Cromelin that it was an allegory written in a Biblical argot, and that he was "very fond of that lyric," a comment quickly qualified by claiming he wasn't "totally satisfied with how the actual track came out."

# Aja

ABC ABCL 5225, September 1977; current LP MCA MCL 1745 (1983),
CD MCAD 37214 (1984)

**R**ELEASED IN **SEPTEMBER 1977,** *AJA* WAS **STEELY DAN'S** MASTERPIECE. **ABC** HAD been jockeying around all summer waiting for exactly the right moment to release the album, attempting to avoid a clash with any other big acts. Ironically, after all that, it came out on the same day as The Rolling Stones' disappointing *Love You Live.*

*Aja* garnered $1,000,000 worth of advance orders, chalked up sales of 5,000,000, fired into the top three of the US album chart and stayed there for more than a year. It also went top five in the UK without the benefit of a hit single, an even more remarkable achievement.

And all this while ABC were hassling Becker and Fagen into releasing two albums in order to complete their contract (they wanted to move over to Warner Brothers), imposing deadlines, and threatening all manner of legal consequences if these deadlines weren't met. Becker even stated publicly at one point that ABC had threatened to confiscate their master tapes if their demands weren't met. Fortunately, this never came to pass.

The majority of recording and overdubbing was done in Los Angeles with that familiar set of musicians, Purdie, Carlton, Omartian, Rainey and Parks. The last song, 'Peg', was recorded in New York while the rest of the LP was being remixed. On *Aja*, Becker and Fagen went back to more complex jazz harmony, and their compositional vision meant that they would be thinking about a particular solo and player very early on in its conception, and structuring each song with that firmly in mind. By the same token, many musicians had enough experience of Steely Dan sessions to know instinctively what Becker and Fagen liked and expected from them. A combination of these two elements helped create a sonically superb, musically masterful, and lyrically lustrous album.

In fact, Becker and Fagen were obviously delighted with their efforts, since they even considered touring again soon after its release. The same very expensive studio players who helped record it were contacted and asked how much they wanted to hit the road with Steely Dan. Since all were invariably earning a fortune as session players, their requirements were of the order of the proverbial king's ransom. Becker and Fagen hand-picked a seven foot Yamaha Piano to take on the road, and Fagen allegedly composed a 45-minute medley for the tour. Rehearsals started in Denny Dias' house, but when certain musicians realised there was a "sliding pay scale" which they were on the lower end of, the arguments started and Becker and Fagen promptly canned the idea.

Steely Dan in 1972, left to right: Jim Hodder, David Palmer,
Denny Dias, Donald Fagen, Jeff Baxter and Walter Becker.
*(Michael Ochs Archive/Redferns)*

David Palmer, front, with – left to right – Jeff Baxter, Walter Becker,
Denny Dias, Donald Fagen and Jim Hodder.
*(Michael Ochs Archive/Redferns)*

The Dan with their gold albums for *Can't Buy A Thrill* (1972) (inset).
*(Michael Ochs Archive/Redferns)*

*Countdown To Ecstasy* (1973)

*Pretzel Logic* (1974)

Steely Dan at home – in the studio. *(Michael Ochs Archive/Redferns)*

Donald and Walter in 1975. *(Michael Ochs Archive/Redferns)*

*Katy Lied* (1975)

*The Royal Scam* (1976)

Donald and Walter in 1976, by which time they had 'become' Steely Dan by virtue of firing everyone else and taking on session musicians with each new record. *(Michael Ochs Archive/Redferns)*

*Aja* (1977)

*Gaucho* (1980)

Donald Fagen, keyboards and vocals. *(LFI)*

*Steely Dan Gold* (1982)

The reformed group on stage at New York's Roseland Ballroom
in October, 1995. *(LFI)*

Walter (left) and Donald at Roseland. *(LFI)*

Donald on stage at Roseland. *(LFI)*

The packaging of the album – fronted by an enigmatic photograph of a Japanese model by Hideki Fuji in an expensive liquid lam finish and featuring a full song-by-song musician listing, lyrics, and sleeve notes which testified to Becker and Fagen's irritability – matched the quality of the music, *Aja* was the ultimate aural experience.

A newcomer to Steely Dan sessions was the sax player and arranger, Tom Scott. Becker and Fagen hired him to write all the horn arrangements for the album, and they were more than pleased with the way things turned out. Because of the complex harmonies, Scott used five saxes, two trombones and a trumpet. In the wake of *Aja*'s release, Becker and Fagen let Denny Dias go (he had been kept on the payroll as a sort of salaried consultant in the meantime), hired Irving Azoff as their manager after considerable encouragement from Gary Katz, and, lo and behold, within days Fagen was back in the recording studio with Paul Griffin working on yet more new tunes. Roger Nichols won a Grammy for Best Engineered Recording.

## BLACK COW

ALMOST the perfect introduction, 'Black Cow' sets a detached mood for Steely Dan's sixth studio album. Fagen stated at one point that the setting for the song was a non-descript luncheonette (probably in Brooklyn) which serves Black Cow, a cocktail which is the subject's chosen method of obliterating the sorrow she feels as she faces the inevitable fact that her relationship is over.

Joe Sample's clavinet croaks in unison with Chuck Rainey's lubricious bass, Fagen's voice is at its most hip, while the girls' serene background vocals suggest reconciliation rather than retribution. Tom Scott's wilting sax break takes us to the fade – the trouble is you never want it to end.

## AJA

THIS seven-minute 56-second suite was put together using a variety of bits and pieces which Fagen had lying around in his head, and which he'd not yet succeeded in using. One of these was a song intriguingly called 'Stand By The Sea Wall'. According to Becker, Fagen once claimed to have known a Korean girl called Aja, but even his writing partner didn't believe him.

Becker and Fagen envisioned rehearsing it for a day, because when the musicians entered the studio, they were faced with seven pages of taxing musical score, but all were fantastic sight readers and the tune was in the can in no time. Primarily this was down to a first time player, drummer Steve Gadd, whose ad-libbed drum solo takes the song to its final lofty plateau.

Denny Dias played another superlative solo and Weather Report saxophonist Wayne Shorter, also making his debut on a Steely Dan record, completed the track with Gadd by way of a 64-bar tenor solo which was pieced together from two separate takes. 'Aja' might perhaps be classified as Steely Dan's own 'Stairway To Heaven'.

## DEACON BLUES

BECKER and Fagen are still particularly proud of this song. Fagen explained "it was a kind of socio-cultural explanation of how we grew up and some of the reasons that people became musicians." It describes how, back in New York in the early to mid-Sixties, both Becker and Fagen were listening to jazz radio stations from Manhattan and visualising an existence, mixing with the nocturnal crowd, making first class music in dingy clubs and bars. (A theme that Fagen chose to explore much more fully on *The Nightfly*).

'Deacon Blues' – edited down from its original seven plus minutes and coupled with 'Home at Last' – became the second single from *Aja* and reached number 19 in April 1978. The sax player was Peter Christlieb, who Becker and Fagen discovered playing after the commercial breaks on *The Tonight Show*. Katz described the tenor player as a "free spirit. You just run the music by him and he blows his brains out." Becker and Fagen later went on to

produce a jazz album by the Pete Christlieb and Warne Marsh Quintet called *Apogee*.

## PEG

THE LAST song to be recorded for the album became its first single, hitting number 11 in November 1977. Rick Marotta, the drummer on 'Peg', said it all when he told Ken Micallef of *Modern Drummer* magazine that "You could have hung your coat up on the groove, created by me and Chuck Rainey." Marotta used a snare drum which originally belonged to Buddy Rich.

The story of the numerous guitarists who tried the guitar solo on 'Peg' has become legend. The one who finally nailed it was a Los Angeles musician called Jay Graydon. Larry Carlton was another who tried it without success, and extracted a form of revenge on Becker and Fagen by using the chords from 'Peg' for his own composition 'Room 335'. Whenever Carlton played it live, he would introduce the song as "The tune I stole from Steely Dan," but he had in fact sought and received their express permission for its use.

Becker and Fagen apparently told Chuck Rainey not to play slap bass – a style that was currently in vogue – as they didn't want to be seen to be jumping on the bandwagon. However, Rainey somewhat resented being told how to play, since he thought himself more than capable of deciding what style most fit the song. When it came time to record, Rainey turned his back to the control room so that Becker and Fagen didn't (or at least pretended not to) notice him slapping.

Prior to Michael McDonald singing the background part, a very well known singer (whom Steely Dan declined to name) tried, but he failed, so Becker, Fagen and Katz resorted to the man who had obliged so often before. 'Peg' was later sampled by hip-hop trio De La Soul for their hit 'Eye Know' in 1989.

## HOME AT LAST

A NOTHER ambitious composition, 'Home At Last' was Becker and Fagen's short take on Homer's *Odyssey* and James Joyce's *Ulysses*. Bernard Purdie executes another perfect shuffle as only he can, and there you have in place the key pieces of this very complex jigsaw. The chorus came from an earlier version of the song.

'Home At Last' is another Steely Dan song which includes references to an unusual drink, this time the Greek wine Retsina, and a close inspection of their lyrics reveals a veritable bar room of exotic drinks.

Rainey is a giant on the bass, and Becker solos with all the languid grace of an uncoiling python.

## I GOT THE NEWS

'I GOT THE News' was originally written for *Katy Lied*. By the time it got recorded for *Aja*, the lyric had taken on an overtly sexual tone; having been reconstructed, primarily for Victor Feldman's piano part, which is liberally sprinkled throughout the tune. What was then the third verse now provided the song's opening lines, while other telling phrases such as "Daddy is a rare millionaire" and "all the sirens and the band get to bending my ear" were retained. This is drummer Ed Greene's only appearance on a Steely Dan album and what an incredibly busy one it is. Michael McDonald's voice soars and swoops like a lark on the wing.

## JOSIE

'J OSIE' was the third single to be taken from Aja, backed by 'Black Cow', reaching number 26 in September 1978, a full year after the album's release. It marked another debut of an auspicious player, drummer Jim Keltner, who took the chair but also wound up playing a dustbin lid on the tune, hence his credit for percussion. Chuck Rainey's serpentine bass line gives the song its funky stretched feeling.

Josie is a revered female anti-hero – a street fighting, law breaking good time girl with a loyal band of followers, all of whom are outside the law. The song contains an allusion to the Charlie Parker song 'Scrapple From The Apple' in the second verse.

# Gaucho

MCA MCF 3090 November 1980; current LP MCA MCF 3090
CD MCAD 37220 (1984) & MCA DIDX 56 (1985)

**T**HE THREE YEARS BETWEEN THE RELEASE OF *AJA* AND *GAUCHO* WERE FULL of incident: Becker and Fagen had taken a year off from their exertions and moved back to the same apartment building in New York, Becker's long time girlfriend, Karen Stanley, had died in Becker's apartment, Becker himself broke his leg in a car accident, and the band's lengthy recording schedules had grown ever more torturous. Between eight months and a year was spent in trying to lay down basic tracks for the album.

Then manager, Irving Azoff, had claimed that Steely Dan were owed several million dollars in unpaid royalties by ABC, who, in the meantime, had been taken over by MCA who claimed that it wasn't their responsibility. Becker and Fagen wanted to put the LP out on Warner Bros but after various court hearings, MCA were finally awarded the album and an agreement was reached to get it in the shops in time for Christmas 1980 which would obviously benefit both parties. When it was finally released, *Gaucho* was the most expensive non-soundtrack album in American history, and Becker and Fagen's attempts to limit the retail price had failed.

For *Gaucho*, the pair would book a band for a couple of nights, fail to get any acceptable tracks, call in another band for a further two nights... and so the process went on. Roger Nichols was keen for Becker and Fagen to try digital recording, but after an initial investigation and a Soundstream demonstration, they decided to stick with analog methods (using up 360 2-inch rolls of tape).

Steely Dan also suffered their most serious set-back when a recording engineer inadvertently erased a completed song called 'The Second Arrangement' which, at the time, was Gary Katz's favourite song on the album. Although they spent $60,000 trying to re-record the song, it never jelled as well again, and was shelved.

Since Becker and Fagen's desire for an absolutely perfect drum track was causing them such frustration and delay, Nichols took it upon himself to design and build a drum machine. Working every spare moment, he came up with an 8-bit machine he called 'Wendel' which could emulate all the inflections of a human drummer. Although the computer did play quite extensively on the album, the live drummer receives full credit in each case, with 'Wendel' being relegated to the sidelines, under "Sequencing and Special Effects."

On the keyboard front, *Gaucho* employed electric pianos and synthesisers in preference to (or in addition to) acoustic pianos, which Fagen denied was an intended stylistic shift, and which he attributed simply to a lack of good sounding pianos in the studios of their choice.

The studio credits on *Gaucho* reflected the difficulties in recording; sessions took place at A&R, Sigma Sound, Soundworks and Automated Sound in New York, as well as the Village Recorders and Producers Workshop in Los Angeles. Following in *Aja*'s footsteps, *Gaucho* went platinum, and Nichols won his third Grammy in five years for best engineered album. However, seven months after the release of the album, it was announced that Becker and Fagen had dissolved their long standing partnership. Fagen intended to make a solo album; Becker intended to look for production projects and to kick his drug habit.

Yet another superb cover fronted the album. Frenchman Rene Burri photographed a mural in the La Boca district of Buenos Aires, depicting a couple doing the tango. Dancing was a way of life for Gauchos, and they often danced in the streets. New York Art Director Susanne Walsh found the photograph in Burri's book about Gauchos and it was absolutely perfect for the album.

---

## BABYLON SISTERS

"I DON'T know how many songs we've written about whores. It must be every other one. It's all very deliberate," Walter Becker said in 1981. 'Babylon Sisters' certainly fits into that category; another tale of the Hollywood high life, with a sparse groove driven along by Bernard Purdie and Chuck Rainey, and the horn section stabbing into the song like a crazed butcher. Becker and Fagen played no instruments on the song, but spent three weeks trying to mix it. Despite all their tracking problems, 'Babylon Sisters' was a second take. As Steve Khan once said, "When Bernard Purdie puts his hat and coat on and says 'that's it', that's it, even for Becker and Fagen."

The story tells of a man who has lost his sexual potency and who seeks to try to regain it by hiring a couple of exotic prostitutes for a threesome. Don Grolnick's Rhodes piano lends it an almost spooky atmosphere.

---

## HEY NINETEEN

LIKE 'Babylon Sisters', 'Hey Nineteen' posed an awful lot of problems for Becker and Fagen. They couldn't get a track they were happy with, and so ended up stripping it down to just Rick Marotta's drum track and overdubbing everything else. Fagen said they were looking for a "kind of mechanical rhythm and blues", a sound which they succeeded in finding, but which does seem somewhat mechanical. The song is about an attempted generation gap pick-up, in which the girl doesn't even know who "'Retha Franklin" is. (When Steely Dan later toured, Fagen started substituting the Queen of Soul with Otis Redding).

The one thing the two do have in common is a taste for strong drink and exotic drugs. Fagen is surely acting the part when he asserts "Skate a little lower now." 'Hey Nineteen' was the first single to be released from the LP and was backed by a previously unreleased live version of 'Bodhisattva' from 1974, complete with Jerome Aniton's heroic, intoxicated verbal introduction of the band that he used to call 'Stevie Dan.'

## GLAMOUR PROFESSION

THE LONGEST song on *Gaucho*, 'Glamour Profession' contained an old chorus which the Becker and Fagen had written while still at college. Fagen admitted that the bridge was a take on Kurt Weill's 'Speak Low' and had been influenced by disco music. A mellow and sweet sounding composition on the face of it, 'Glamour Profession' depicts a high flying basketball star who can't leave cocaine alone, and his supplier who is almost as wealthy, and who feels as much of a star as his client. The character's name, Hoops McCann, inspired an all-star jazz band to name themselves after him, and do an entire album of Steely Dan covers.

## GAUCHO

SOON after its release, the title track came back to haunt Becker and Fagen when it became clear that they had 'borrowed' the introductory melody from Jan Garbarek and Keith Jarrett's 1974 song 'Long As You Know You're Living Yours.' When a musician journalist raised a question about the similarity, they eventually admitted to being "heavily influenced by that particular piece of music", and later approved their off-the-record response for publication. (Jarrett sued Steely Dan when he became aware of it, and received a co-writing credit on all future pressings of the album.)

The song was another difficult one to nail featuring several pages of score, but was eventually recorded one night, long after Becker and Fagen had given up and gone home, when a band featuring the inevitable Jeff Porcaro, Steve Khan and Victor Feldman, became absolutely determined to achieve an acceptable take, staying in the studio until 5 am. Even then, Becker, Fagen and Gary Katz did some forty odd edits and only kept the drum track, building up from the bottom again.

Renowned for their use of unusual words (sometimes even of their own invention), here Becker and Fagen introduced another two which attracted much critical attention: "bodacious" and "Custerdome". They got their customary laughs and mileage out of explaining these – or not as the case may be – during interviews.

## TIME OUT OF MIND

A TYPICAL Becker and Fagen song, written in Fagen's house in Malibu before they moved back to New York, with more references to drug taking, 'Time Out Of Mind' features a guitar solo from Dire Straits' main man Mark Knopfler. Knopfler later explained how he found it a very trying experience, with Becker and Fagen requiring take after take. As he couldn't read music, Knopfler had to take a tape of the song back to his hotel room to work on it at greater length.

'Time Out Of Mind' was the second single taken from the album, and reached number 22 in America, but not before an argument with Steely Dan and MCA over the latter's decision to once again use the live version of 'Bodhisattva' as the single's B-side. Steely Dan had already agreed that 'Third World Man' should be the flip.

## MY RIVAL

'M Y RIVAL' exemplifies Becker and Fagen's fastidiousness. Rick Derringer worked for hours on the eight-bar intro, but his attempts at the solo didn't gain their approval, and so it fell to Steve Khan to play it. Fagen's instructions to Kahn were that he wanted it to sound like Hubert Sumlin (Howlin' Wolf's guitar player). Khan played it on a Telecaster and Wendel did most of the drum track, although Steve Gadd received the credit.

## THIRD WORLD MAN

'T HIRD World Man' was originally recorded at the *Aja* sessions, under the title 'Were You Blind That Day?' described by Fagen in 1977 as a Third World fantasy. When they needed a song to finish the album, Becker and Fagen pulled it from the vaults, re-wrote the lyrics, kept Larry Carlton's sublime solo and built up a whole new song about a disturbed boy who, if he succeeds in attaining adulthood, will certainly make a Rambo-type character.

# Two Against Nature

Giant 74321 62190-2, February 2000

**S**TEELY **D**AN **RELEASED SEVEN CRITICALLY ACCLAIMED ALBUMS BETWEEN** 1972-1980 but announced their split to Robert Palmer in the *New York Times* in June 1981. There was no animosity involved. Walter Becker went to live in Maui, got married and started a family but still kept in intermittent touch with his erstwhile partner. They even wrote the occasional song together by phone/fax.

In the latter part of the Nineties, when interviewed about various outside projects, the inevitable question about any possible Steely Dan reunion arose. Fagen spent a good deal of time denying that the band as an entity existed any longer. "They're gone", he'd say, as if an outsider looking in.

However, after meeting and marrying Libby Titus and being persuaded to play New York clubs on a restrained level, gradually the interest increased and Steely Dan began to be reformed by stealth, almost unbeknownst to Becker and Fagen themselves.

Following the Art Crimes tour of 1996, Steely Dan were back in the studio having resolved that if they were going to resume their career, they should do it wholeheartedly. Walter Becker had fathered a son and daughter, divorced his wife and was now splitting his time between Maui and New York. Their songwriting partnership reactivated, he and Fagen were seen taking walks around New York City, looking for inspiration and occasionally to escape the frustration of a non-productive day's work.

If anything, Becker and Fagen found songwriting harder in the late Nineties as their standards were even higher than during the Seventies. The pair spent the best part of a year writing, then began recording at Fagen and Gary Katz' River Sound (since closed down), Clinton and Electric Lady studios in the city and at Becker's home studio, Hyperbolic Sound in Maui.

The pair intended to make the record on tape and do simple editing using two machines but they soon discovered this was going to take ten times as long to do and switched to digital audio software. Steely Dan were at last back in business; hiring and firing musicians (they used six drummers on only nine songs) switching from studio to studio – just like their heyday. They built up each track starting with live drums, then electric piano, bass, guitars and finally the vocals/horns/background vocals.

As had so often been the case *Two Against Nature* was very well received by the critics and charted at number 6 on *Billboard*, being registered platinum within four months of its release. Steely Dan's Y2K tour hit the road in May beginning in Japan, then USA and Europe, winding up in Germany in September.

---

## GASLIGHTING ABBIE

THE FIRST song on the album had been inspired by the 1944 Charles Boyer/Ingrid Bergman film, *Gaslight* (UK title: *The Murder at Thornton Square*). Becker and Fagen changed the noun to a verb and explained that "to gaslight" some-one was New York slang – a synonym for mind-fucking. In the movie, playing a Victorian schizophrenic, Boyer tries to drive Bergman insane by turning the lights on and off and moving items of clothing around, etc. In the song, Yellowjackets' drummer Ricky Lawson and Tom Barney lock in together as though the game could go on forever and Becker and Fagen even slip in 'Cara Mia' – a sly lyrical reference to their Jay and the Americans past.

## WHAT A SHAME ABOUT ME

ALL STEELY Dan albums contain an "altered blues" and *Two Against Nature* is no exception. 'What A Shame About Me' is almost a novel-la – a story about a self-pitying, down-and-out protagonist who works a day-job at the Strand book-store on Broadway and who encounters an old flame, Franny, who has become quite a celebrity in the intervening years. He's embar-rassed by how successful she (and all of his old acquaintances) have become and so declines her offer of casual sex. Walter Becker decorates the track with serpentine bass lines and guitar noodles.

## TWO AGAINST NATURE

THE TITLE song is the grisliest of gruesome dreams – a 21st centu-ry look at voodoo, taking the premise of a Haitian Divorce several stages further. Becker told *The Guardian*'s Barney Hoskyns "it's about the songwriters' invocation of their own powers to overcome the natural and supernatural forces arrayed against them. They're offer-ing to help their audience prevail in the face of all sorts of mysterious and frightening beings."

'Two Against Nature' marks the first appearance of drummer Keith Carlock who, contrary to his own impression, had impressed Becker and Fagen although they didn't use all of his work for the album. This is the only song on which the pair used a sequence to trigger a bass synth. Becker and Fagen borrowed the word "grok" from Robert Heinlein's book *Stranger In A Strange Land* and, never ones to shirk a challenge, invented and included one of their own: "apsatively."

## JANIE RUNAWAY

BECKER and Fagen tried several names (Dixie, Molly, Annie) for this snappy tale of a teenage Tampa absconder. It was rejected by one radio station as a focus track because it featured a sax solo. The station informed the record company "we only play songs with guitar solos." This prompted an outraged Fagen to comment that you could write a song about fucking your grandmother [and get airtime] as long as it had a guitar solo. But in this case it wasn't a grandmother they had in mind; Fagen's husky and suggestive vocals urge the under-age nymphet to decamp with him for a dirty weekend. Little does she know, she's going with him whether she likes it or not. Janie Runaway contains a lyrical nod, "I'm painting again" to one of Fagen's favourite songs – Talking Heads' 'Artists Only' from 1978's *More Songs About Buildings And Food*.

## ALMOST GOTHIC

A TRULY lovely song about a creature of rash contradictions – perfectly exemplified by the fact that one instant she's the tiny and innocent babysitter for Carole King who went on to have a hit with 'The Locomotion', the next she's a genuinely objectionable "Bleecker Street brat". Nonetheless, he's totally smitten and has a real bad case of subterranean lovesick blues.

Michael Leonhart's melancholy trumpet solo alludes to the dark place in the lyrics.

## JACK OF SPEED

AN UNFORTUNATE disappointment. When Steely Dan played this song during their 1996 tour, the horns had much more snap and vitality and drove the action along. For the recorded version, they slowed it down, changed the key, Donald Fagen took over on vocals and the lyrics were altered in places. Michael White's snare drum sound resembles a wet lettuce being struck and Walter Becker's guitar solo lacks fluidity in this song about the personification of demonic obsession.

## COUSIN DUPREE

A MINOR hit single, Becker and Fagen had this song lying around for a while prior to *Two Against Nature*. The album's equivalent to 'New Frontier' and 'Tomorrow's Girls,' with the commerciality not even remotely masking a tale of a sexual wolf who has taken a fancy to his younger cousin. Becker plays a leering and lascivious guitar solo as only he could, Leroy Clouden punches the track along like a champion middleweight and Fagen's stepdaughter, Amy Helm, gets in on the act whistling over the bridge. The songwriters intended this to have a Chuck Berry-type quality, while, at the same time, being a parody of a country song.

## NEGATIVE GIRL

ON THE face of it, 'Negative Girl' seems light and airy, almost detached, but Donald Fagen described the final two songs on the album as "a pretty dense pair of tracks". Tom Barney's bass is indubitably dense, while drummer Vinnie Colauita lends the song its breezy feel and Dave Schenk's vibe solo teeters on the edge of mystery, which is remarkable since this was a second take. Becker and Fagen did not play on this track at all.

## WEST OF HOLLYWOOD

AT 8:21, the longest ever Steely Dan studio song, 'West Of Hollywood' could be the precursor to what would become the title song of Two Against Nature's follow up, Everything Must Go. Earth Wind and Fire's Sonny Emory is the sixth drummer to feature and the last four minutes of the song are dedicated to Chris Potter's tenor sax solo. Potter said in order to achieve the effect they were looking for Becker and Fagen suggested that before one of his passes, he should think about John Coltrane's 'Sheets Of Sound'.

"We just couldn't shake him. He seemed prepared to improvise soulfully and swingingly over any kind of chords we gave him." Becker also said it "had a Heart Of Darkness [Joseph Conrad novel] thing going on." Fagen simply said it had an "apocalyptic quality." This was another old song which had had a reggae-type feel but which had never been set to lyrics.

# Everything Must Go

Reprise CDW 48435, June 2003

**F**OLLOWING THE RELEASE OF **TWO AGAINST NATURE**, **A HOST OF PLAUDITS WAS** to come Becker and Fagen's way. In May 2000 they were honoured by ASCAP with the Founders Award for a lifetime achievement in songwriting. Fully a year after its release *Two Against Nature* won a Grammy for Album of the Year. In March 2001 Becker and Fagen were inducted into the Rock n' Roll Hall of Fame and in May of that year they were given Honorary Doctor of Music degrees at Boston's Berklee College of Music. Becker and Fagen attended the ceremony where versions of Steely Dan songs were performed by selected students. The duo later shook hands with 600 of the attendees.

On September 11, New York was hit by the attacks on the World Trade Center while Becker and Fagen were recording *Everything Must Go*, but as the songs had already been written, the outrage didn't really have a bearing on the album, although both 'The Last Mall' and 'GodWhacker' took on an altogether more portentous quality.

Much of the recording was done at Sear Sound (formerly the Hit Factory), the studio where Becker and Fagen had recorded Terence Boylan's *Alias Boona* album back in 1969. It was a small, old fashioned studio but the duo loved the way it sounded and renowned engineer Elliott Scheiner persuaded them to record the album in analog. Becker and Fagen's idea was to try and get complete performances which required the musicians to have a completely different mindset from a hitherto typical Steely Dan session. This involved spending a day familiarising themselves with the songs then recording them in batches of two or three at a time. It's ironic that Steely Dan spent the Seventies frequently lamenting that technology wasn't advanced enough to enable them to do increasingly difficult recording, then some 30 years later when the machinery *had* caught up, they should step back to traditional methods for a richer and warmer sound.

Unfortunately sporting the same title as a best-selling Manic Street Preachers' album, *Everything Must Go* contained mostly short songs with a total running time of only 42 minutes and only one drummer! The Charles Gullung-staged photograph of a New York street trader with a briefcase full of watches and necklaces was both predictable and unimaginative by Steely Dan standards.

## THE LAST MALL

IF SOMEONE had told a Steely Dan fan, around the time of *The Royal Scam*, that Becker and Fagen would open a song – let alone an album – with the line "Attention all shoppers", they would have gaped in sheer disbelief. 'The Last Mall' is a fairly unremarkable song rescued by Fagen's angular horn arrangement. It doesn't sound like an opener and would have been better served further down the list of songs. (Fagen dubbed it "Apocalyse Wow"). The story being told is of a final trip for some retail therapy before Armageddon hits. The song ends abruptly perhaps indicating that the end of the world scenario has finally happened.

## THINGS I MISS THE MOST

ALTHOUGH Becker and Fagen disguised this song with comments about poking fun at Yuppies with their "good copper pans", "the Audi TT", and "comfy Eames chair" this is basically an autobiographical song about Becker's divorce from his wife Elinor. Fagen does a good job of portraying his partner's sorrow via a compassionate vocal.

## BLUES BEACH

'BLUES Beach', with its "plink-plonk" opening, was an early single taken from the album. As Fagen had invented a car he dubbed "the Kamakiri" for his second solo album, he and Becker came up with a "paranymphic glider" – an imaginary vehicle for an imaginary girl and an imaginary date. A respectful nod to the late Laura Nyro with the reference to a "stone[d] soul picnic" was given and indeed, throughout the album, several classic song titles were lyrically referenced including 'Knock On Wood' and 'Duke Of Earl' ('Slang Of Ages') and 'Wouldn't It Be Nice?' ('Everything Must Go'). The vocal interplay between Fagen and Carolyn Leonhart on the fadeout encourages the listener to leave town and head off to Blues Beach – that special place where all your troubles disappear.

## GODWHACKER

IN THE WAKE of 9/11, this song had commentators speculating as to the identity of the GodWhacker. Becker and Fagen vigorously denied that the subject was George W. Bush, but a close inspection of the lyrics reveals the capital W indicated that "Double-yuh" may have been more than just a shadow looming large behind this song. Becker and Fagen also mention a "Western deity" and "Mr Big". 'GodWhacker' has a great Keith Carlock groove and Fagen executes a nice synth solo with a melodica sound from a Korg Triton which is answered by Becker's 'out-of-whack' guitar solo.

## SLANG OF AGES

WALTER Becker's first lead vocal on a Steely Dan song; joking that he had put it off until the last possible moment. This exercise in wordplay, suited his limited vocal range which, cloaked by five background singers, is wanton and lustful, improving on his *Eleven Tracks Of Whack* vocal efforts. Becker also contributes a very precise and fiendish bass sound.

## GREEN BOOK

THINGS start really cooking by track six. The film noir-ish 'Green Book' has everything: Carlock goes into groove mode again; Ted Baker runs through some *Aja*-esque piano between the verses; a mercurial Becker guitar solo and his five-string bass played through an envelope filter; a crafty-as-a-fox Fagen synthesiser solo and an enigmatic, name-dropping lyric that could allude to anything.

"We imagined a pornography beyond online porn," explained Becker. "A pornography involving some sort of magical remote viewing that flirts somewhere on the borderline of jealousy and intense arousal."

## PIXELEEN

THIS seems to be a composite of a character from a computer game/video/low-budget movie with "sleek and soulful cyberqueen" Carolyn Leonhart's wonderful featured background vocal enhancements. Walter Becker plays his tastiest bass on the album; the chink-chink rhythm guitar part is wholly appropriate and Walt Weiskopf's sax solo is contagious. Becker explained that it was Bill Charlap who had come up with something really surprising: "Every once in a while, we get something that falls apart in a nice way. That is one of them."

## LUNCH WITH GINA

AS WITH so many Becker and Fagen songs, 'Lunch With Gina' is about a psychologically disturbed female, similar to the Glenn Close-type character from the Adrian Lyne-directed *Fatal Attraction*. Donald Fagen plays a fittingly deranged and strident synth solo in the middle and on the fadeout.

## EVERYTHING MUST GO

WALTER Becker commented that he and Becker had wanted to write a song about business for some time, but had never quite got it right. 'Everything Must Go' seems to be an Enron-type quagmire of fraud, false accounting, sexual shenanigans and 'jobs-for-the-boys', but the duo also described it as being "a song about a bunch of losers." They also admitted it was a comment on stores who held "closing down" sales which were no more than an outright con. The track originally had a piano introduction, but when the duo heard Walt Weiskopf's street jazz sound they appropriated that for the long intro. Carlock's snare drum sound has a bite to it and whereas in the Seventies, Steely Dan would simply have hired the late Don Grolnick for the clavinet part, this time Fagen took it on and acquitted himself exceedingly well.

# DONALD FAGEN
## The Nightfly

Warner Bros 92-3696-2 October 1982
Current LP WB 9236961 (1982) & W3696 (1982), CD WB 92 3696 2 (1983)

**E**VEN AS STEELY DAN WERE IN THE THROES OF THEIR SPLIT, DONALD FAGEN was forming the idea of an autobiographical album set in the late Fifties and early Sixties when he was growing up in New Jersey. Having taken eight months to write and a similar amount of time to record, *The Nightfly* was released in October 1982 on the Warner Bros label. Fagen utilised virtually the same Steely Dan session names with Gary Katz and Roger Nichols in their respective production/engineering roles.

The critics promptly (and unfairly) jumped on the question: so what *was* Walter Becker's contribution to Steely Dan? Fagen had written all the songs alone, so much of Steely Dan's customary bite and edge was missing, although, as they were composed from a child's point of view, this was Fagen's overall intention. Initially to be called *Talk Radio*, *The Nightfly* contained seven Fagen originals and a cover of Leiber/Stoller's 'Ruby Baby', originally done by The Drifters in 1956.

The album peaked at number 11 in America, aided by the first single 'I.G.Y. (What A Beautiful World)' which hit number 26 the same month (November 1982). It didn't fare nearly as well in the UK, reaching only 44, and despite fairly heavy airplay, all three singles missed out on UK chart success.

Fagen wrote six of the tunes pretty easily, but had considerable trouble finishing enough songs to complete the album. In an *Off The Record* interview at the time, he hinted at the future difficulties which would confront him when stating that he'd slowly been losing interest in writing and recording, somehow feeling he should be finished as soon as he got the idea, with only the impetus gained from great studio performances to keep him going.

Over seven Steely Dan albums Becker and Fagen had never been pictured on the sleeve, but Fagen broke that tradition with *The Nightfly*. Photographer James Hamilton staged a mock up of a Fifties radio studio in Fagen's apartment, showing Fagen posed at the turntable and microphone, smoking Chesterfields, spinning a Sonny Rollins record.

After the brief flirtation with digital recording on *Gaucho*, Fagen got firmly behind Roger Nichols to record the album on 32 track and 4 track 3M digital machines, but as the machines were new, they often broke down. One alignment problem they encountered eventually meant that Nichols, Jerry Garsszva and Wayne Yurgelun had to travel to Minnesota to acquire the know-how to deal with the problem themselves.

A few years on from the first 'Wendel', Nichols updated it to sixteen bits as opposed to the original's eight. Elliot Scheiner recorded the basic tracks in Los Angeles and Daniel Lazerus was brought in to engineer the album. However, after this considerable high tech studio wizardry had been employed, when the CD came out, Nichols received a call from, of all people, Stevie Wonder, who told him that the disc sounded "funny". When Nichols checked it, he discovered that the CD sounded inferior to the analog vinyl album. Third and even fourth generation masters were routinely being used to manufacture compact discs, and Nichols wrote a detailed article in the December issue of *Recording Engineer And Producer* demanding that record companies tighten up on their downright careless attitude to their artists' material.

One significant difference on *The Nightfly* was that Fagen moved away from getting the rhythm section together with the studio, preferring to build up the tracks layer by layer.

The album was nominated for seven Grammies: LP of the Year; Song of the Year for 'IGY'; Best Pop Vocal; Best Instrumental Arrangement with a Vocal; Best Vocal arranged for two or more voices; Best Engineered Album; and Producer of the Year, Gary Katz.

---

## I.G.Y. (WHAT A BEAUTIFUL WORLD)

'I.G.Y.' WAS short for International Geophysical Year, which ran from July 1957 to December 1958 and involved widespread scientific co-operation and research between nations. Bearing in mind the period, and the great emphasis on technology for the future, Fagen wanted to include a song which showed how that heady optimism was rapidly dashed in reality.

'I.G.Y.' was lifted as the first single and charted at number 26 in America.

Walter on stage at Brussells, September 1996. *(LFI)*

Donald on stage at Brussells, 1996. *(LFI)*

*Citizen Steely Dan*, the group's
4-CD box set (1993)

*Alive in America* (1995)

On stage in Holland. *(LFI)*

*Android Warehouse* (1998)

Donald in Brussells, September 1996. *(LFI)*

Walter and Donald collect their Ascap Awards at the Beverly Hilton Hotel, Los Angeles, May 2000. *(Steve Granitz/Retna)*

*Two Against Nature* (2000)

*The Steely Dan Story 1972-1980*

Donald and Walter collect Grammy Awards, February, 2001.
*(Steve Granitz/WireImage)*

Donald and Walter at the Rock And Roll Hall of Fame Awards
in New York, March 2001. *(LFI)*

*Everything Must Go* (2003)

Donald on stage at the R'n'R Hall of Fame Awards. *(LFI)*

Walter Becker and Donald Fagen in 2002. *(Emily Wilson/Retna)*

## GREEN FLOWER STREET

'GREEN Flower Street' became a firm favourite on the live circuit once Steely Dan resumed touring in the Nineties. It's a Chinatown romance, which was perhaps inspired by the jazz standard 'On Green Dolphin Street', and contains the underlying threat of violence which often accompanies a Steely Dan and/or Fagen love song.

The rhythm section of Jeff Porcaro and Chuck Rainey were reunited and the song boasts no less than three guitarists and three keyboard players.

## RUBY BABY

THIS Leiber/Stoller song, already 27 years old when Fagen (who liked the innocence of the song's lyrics) came to record it, posed the recording team yet more problems. Michael Omartian and Greg Phillinganes ended up seated at the same piano, playing the high and low parts respectively. Phillinganes then played the solo, taking The Kinks' 'You Really Got Me' as inspiration, but somehow the piano was out of tune with the synthesisers when they were later added. Fagen refused to dispense with Phillinganes' solo, so Nichols and company took the song apart in order to fit in the synths around the piano.

The Drifters' original probably took about one tenth of the time Fagen's version did to record, but Leiber and Stoller liked his arrangement of their tune. Fagen envisaged a big rhythm and blues party-like arrangement, and, as the recording studio was next door to Studio 54, they tried recording one of Jerry Rubin's parties, but it sounded like a stadium sound, so they actually threw a party in the recording studio, and that's what you hear as the song fades out. Fagen got drunk and wound up standing on a chair encouraging and conducting the assorted party goers.

## MAXINE

'MAXINE' was one of Fagen's great re-writes. Having failed to succeed in recording another song scheduled for the album, he salvaged Ed Greene's drum track and re-wrote a completely new song around it. It's a straightforward song about the perceived idealism of high school romance and teenage love, wrapped in Four Freshmen-style vocal harmonies.

## NEW FRONTIER

STEELY Dan had briefly examined the subject of nuclear war in 'King Of The World' in 1973, and Fagen decided to take another look with this song about a party in a fall-out shelter. Larry Carlton again provided tasty lead guitar; Ed Greene, the foundation; and Hugh McCracken, the bluesy harmonica.

It became the second single and in a surprising move, Fagen hired Cucumber Studios in England to make a promotional video clip which combined live action and animation to good effect. He didn't appear in the video himself, preferring to use a look-alike.

## THE NIGHTFLY

THE PREMISE of the title track is a late night jazz jock broadcasting from Baton Rouge, Louisiana (although it's obviously also based on Fagen's adolescent DJ heroes Mort Fega and Symphony Sid from New York). The lyrics use images from the blues, such as "From the foot of Mount Belzoni" taken from "When the trials in Belzoni/No need to scream and cry", while "Patton's Kiss and Tell" refers to Charley Patton, the Delta blues guitarist.

This song was another ordeal for Michael Omartian because Fagen had him in the studio alone playing along to nothing more than a "nauseating quarter note click track." After hours of this, Omartian was fit to explode but, following subtle placation by Fagen, he managed to gather himself together to capture what was required. 'The Nightfly' was used by UK broadcaster Tommy Vance on his satellite TV show.

## THE GOODBYE LOOK

SET ON a Caribbean island in the Sixties, and inspired by Fagen's love of bossa nova 'The Goodbye Look' is about unrest and upheaval in one such nation. The narrator was reluctant to leave, but now that he has been betrayed by his sweetheart, he must make some hasty arrangements and go before it's too late.

## WALK BETWEEN RAINDROPS

THE FINAL track was based on an old Jewish folk tale about a rabbi/magician who could perform the remarkable feat of the title. Appropriately enough, it was the last song to be recorded, and featured Fagen playing a funky sounding organ – although the funkiness wasn't entirely due to his technique, but more to the fact that the instrument was broken.

Greg Phillinganes' keyboard bass line was doubled by Will Lee in an attempt to achieve the plucked sound of an upright double bass. The "Oh Miami" exclamation was Daniel Lazerus' idea, and Fagen, Katz and Lazerus mimicked similar interjections from old rock and roll records.

# Kamakiriad

Reprise 9362-45230-2, May 1993; reissued in 1993 as Reprise 9362 45230 1, CD 9362 45230-2 (1993)

**G**ETTING ON FOR ELEVEN YEARS AFTER *THE NIGHTFLY* AND AFTER considerable mental anguish and psychological torture due to writer's block, Donald Fagen finally delivered a follow up. Like its predecessor, *Kamakiriad* was an album of connected songs, but this time Fagen told a linear story about an incident packed journey in a steam driven car. When looking for an apt name for this vehicle, he leafed through a Japanese/English Dictionary and came up with the word 'Kamakiri' (meaning preying mantis), which he thought sounded good.

As both Becker and Fagen auditioned their new material in the car (reasoning if it sounds good there, it sounds good anywhere) Fagen specifically wanted *Kamakiriad* to have that driving vibe.

Fagen's original intention was to produce the album himself, but at the last minute he called his partner and installed him as producer. Fagen came to the realisation that it would be easier if Becker played all the bass and guitar parts as well. Recording began as early as May 1990 at the Hit Factory in New York, but soon afterwards Fagen and Gary Katz established their own studio, River Sound, on New York's Upper East Side, where the majority of the recording was done and at Becker's own Hyperbolic Sound in Maui. Much media interest surrounded the duo's return to the studio, but both were at pains to stress that this was *not* a Steely Dan project.

Due to family concerns, recording would take place for four to six weeks at a time, with each member returning home between sessions to recharge. As he had written most of the songs while he was "researching" the New York Rock and Soul Revue, Fagen admitted that the album was heavily influenced by Sixties soul and Seventies funk – from Sly Stone to Earth Wind and Fire.

Fagen would come in with each tune mapped out exactly as he wanted it. Drum sequencing equipment enabled him to set very precise grooves which he wanted the drummer to replicate, and DX bass parts and DX seven rhythm parts were also sketched in, yet, paradoxically, Fagen admitted he felt manipulated by listening to records where the drum track consisted of someone merely pressing a button. The album was recorded a track at a time, with incredible scrutiny applied to each, making sure that everything fit with what was already there and what was to follow. As a result, *Kamakiriad* sounds somewhat mechanical and aloof, and fails to radiate the warmth and rhythmic flair of Steely Dan.

Walter Becker and Roger Nichols recorded and mixed 11 albums (10 hours of music) for the Windham Hill and Triloka jazz labels in the same amount of time it took to record just drums and piano for two tunes on *Kamakiriad*. (Nichols wrote that they were mixing ten tunes a day, as opposed to ten days per tune with Fagen's project.) *Kamakiriad* was the first album not to have Gary Katz in the producer's chair. Fagen said that "effectively he had been automated out of a job" by the availability of complex home studio equipment, but did give Katz credit in his sleeve notes as first on a list of "enablers".

---

## TRANS-ISLAND SKYWAY

FAGEN'S narrator takes delivery of his new car; which has a self-sufficient vegetable garden in the back, a bubble covering the garden, and a link with a navigational satellite called Tripstar. It was a relatively slow moving vehicle – a cosmopolitan construction with the frame coming from Scotland, and the technology from, of all places, Bali – enabling the occupants to take in what was happening around them. The story was set near the end of the century in order to avoid the sentimentality trap. No sooner has the trip begun than the narrator comes across a road side accident, picks up the sexy girl passenger who is unscathed and travels on as the earth's climate and geology throws all it can at them.

The song, which was originally going to be called 'The Trip', for obvious reasons, became the second single, backed by a demo version of 'Big Noise New York' (originally recorded by Jennifer Warnes) and a live version of 'Home At Last' from the Rock and Soul Revue's Beacon Theatre performance from 1991.

## COUNTERMOON

ALWAYS one to look for some opposite viewpoint, Fagen wanted to cast the moon as the bad guy in this song about a moon which makes people fall *out* of love and contemplate much worse acts. It contains Fagen's only solo on the LP, which was based on a saxophone sample. The line "You're not my Jackie" was spoken by Fagen's stepdaughter Amy Helm, daughter of Libby Titus and former Band drummer Levon Helm.

---

## SPRINGTIME

STEELY Dan's buddy Paul Griffin reappears on this track playing some soulful Hammond B3 organ. During the quietly-sung first verse you would hardly recognise that it's Fagen singing, then comes the exclamation "Yowie!" and he's back in full vocal harness. At this juncture, the journeyman visits a kind of sci-fi theme park, where his brain can be scanned for old romances and the memories replayed to him in a virtual reality theatre.

## SNOWBOUND

THIS was the only Becker and Fagen composition to make the final cut and had been written a number of years before Fagen ever had the concept for *Kamakiriad*. Whether or not he had to adapt it in any way to fit with the storyline is not known, but it's a long loping look at the continuous partying of a city in the midst of the frozen wastes. Walter Becker makes a lazy solo last for a full minute.

'Snowbound', released in November 1993, was the third single to be taken from the album, and fared no better in the success stakes than its two predecessors. The CD single was interesting in as much as it contained bass, drums and vocals only mixes of 'Snowbound' and 'Trans-Island Skyway'.

## TOMORROW'S GIRLS

THE MOST commercial song on the album, 'Tomorrow's Girls' was released as the lead single but failed to appear on the charts. It chugs along with Leroy Clouden's hi-hat, and the groove tugs at your sleeve, imploring you to get out on the dancefloor. Basically, it illustrates a sci-fi B movie outline: female aliens invade the earth and take over the minds of the existing girls. Fagen explained that it was a sort of metaphor for waking up after a number of years in a relationship and realising that you and your partner have grown so far apart that she may as well be an alien. (Ironically, perhaps, since Fagen had been married for two years himself by this point.)

## FLORIDA ROOM

LIBBY Titus receives a lyric co-writing credit on this hi-hat/horn fest set in one of Donald Fagen's favourite holiday destinations. It represents the narrator's last chance saloon; if he doesn't succeed in grabbing the slice of happiness on offer here, he is destined for a miserable last few miles on his journey. Woven into the horn bursts are the background vocals, which harness the chorus to each verse and race away to the next rendezvous.

## ON THE DUNES

ORIGINALLY written in 1983, Fagen could not have imagined that it would take over 10 years for 'On The Dunes' to appear on *Kamakiriad*. Becker and Fagen flew Chris Parker out to Maui and spent ten days working on different sounds and tracks. For 'On The Dunes', they set him up in the studio on his own, with almost no verbal indication as to what they wanted, and encouraged him to just keep playing.

The narrator's fellow traveller has now ditched him and the result is an eight minute night time cruise into despair and anxiety, encapsulated by Cornelius Bumpus' sax solo.

## TEAHOUSE ON THE TRACKS

THE FINAL song and the last to be written for the album. The depressed narrator is coming to the end of his journey and is debating whether or not to chuck it all in. He stumbles across the nightclub of the title, and after a vigorous dance session feels rejuvenated, and opts to continue. The track ends up in a similar rhythm and blues workout-party situation like 'Ruby Baby' on *Nightfly*. Bashiri Johnson's trombone solo sounds like a rutting buck.

# WALTER BECKER
## Eleven Tracks Of Whack

Giant 9-24-579.2, September 1994

**W**ALTER BECKER HAD TALKED A LOT ABOUT A SOLO ALBUM DURING interviews to help promote some of his production projects in the early 1990s. He began working in earnest on his debut during the making of *Kamakiriad* and found that his concept of the album drifted as he wrote more and more songs. This creative outpouring ended up with 25 songs for him to choose from in bringing the album in under an hour's duration. Becker's initial reluctance was due to his voice which he didn't feel the public at large was ready for. He considered making an instrumental album before overcoming his vocal doubts and committing himself to a fully fledged album.

Becker realised that he was missing out on the fun of recording his own project when working with Rickie Lee Jones on her 1989 album *Flying Cowboys*. He co-wrote several songs with Dean Parks but only one, 'Cringemaker' made it to the finished album. Recording began with a rhythm section based around the Lost Tribe, whose eponymous album Becker had produced for the Windham Hill Label in 1993, plus keyboardist John Beasley and his erstwhile co-writer Dean Parks. Two weeks was spent recording at Hyperbolic Sound in Maui, during which time three songs ended up on the finished project, followed by additional sessions at LA's Signet Sound. Becker decided to use his original sequenced demos for the rest of the tracks since he felt they contained the real heart of each composition. He admitted he was driving himself nuts by the time Fagen arrived to ease the pressure and to help get him back on track.

The album was released in September 1994 on Irving Azoff's Giant label just as Steely Dan were wrapping up their second successive summer tour. Becker had, in fact, already previewed some of the songs on their 1993 tour but the exodus of the audience whenever they were performed was wryly dubbed the "Procession to the Concession stand" by the composer. Songs like 'Fall Of '92' were eventually dropped.

Just like Fagen's *The Nightfly*, *Eleven Tracks Of Whack* is mostly an autobiographical first solo effort based on assorted acquaintances and Becker's stable family life in Hawaii, a far cry from the low life and exotic characters which populated many Steely Dan songs. However, it still displays Becker's caustic sense of humour and a pre-occupation with the use and abuse of drugs which played a large part in Becker's life for some years. Where Fagen's albums were perfect in sound, production and playing, Becker's is rough-hewn and basic. "Songwriting is a place for me to do some lashing out in a mild sort of way," he said. Becker put a dictionary definition of the word "Whack" on the CD; the second definition being "A first stab or crude attempt" which seemed rather appropriate. Sales were predictably moderate when compared to Steely Dan. The Japanese CD pressing featured a bonus track called "Medical Science".

## DOWN IN THE BOTTOM

SPORTING the same title as a Willie Dixon song and recorded by Howlin' Wolf, 'Down In The Bottom' is a vague reference to a friend of Becker's who was involved in a relationship but who "withheld part of himself in a really obnoxious way." Becker then added various fictitious characters to embellish the story. In one interview he admitted to considering calling the song 'The Dopest Cut'. The prominent drum beat sounds artificial and tends to overwhelm everything else including Becker's own guitar work.

## JUNKIE GIRL

A PROBABLE homage to Karen Stanley, Becker's girlfriend for most of the Seventies and the victim of an overdose in his Manhattan apartment in 1980. Becker was cut up by her death and vigorously defended a lawsuit blaming him for the tragedy by the girl's mother who happened to be a lawyer. Becker not only articulated those old feelings with such heartfelt emotions that he wished perhaps he'd died with her, but is also mightily thankful that he came through his own hell intact. The best song on the album.

## SURF AND/OR DIE

THIS song was based on a real event when a young acquaintance of Becker's was killed in a hang-gliding accident. At his memorial service a group of Tibetan monks spoke very movingly about life and death and Becker was inspired to write a song about it. Later, Becker's wife Elinor invited the monks to the recording studio in order for them to give the song their blessing. Becker recorded their chants, realised it was in the same key as his tribute and used the chants intermittently throughout. Driven by Ben Perowsky's drum, this song with no chorus warmly wraps itself around the listener.

## BOOK OF LIARS

AT LAST the drum machine assault is over and the pace slackens and becomes laid back *a la* Steely Dan. Bob Sheppard's sax calms and soothes over the tale of a girl who just can't say, well, anything really, without lapsing into untruths. This was one of the tunes that Becker debuted on the 1993 Steely Dan tour and which saw a majority crowd exit to get a beer. However, this one survived, while 'Fall of '92' fell by the wayside, eventually appearing on a promo only CD single as a bonus track.

## LUCKY HENRY

A NOTHER Lost Tribe session, but not to be outdone Dean Parks takes the first solo, then Adam Rogers, comes in for the second solo.

## HARD UP CASE

S INISTER sounding from the very first note, 'Hard Up Case' finds Becker's drum machine back on full volume and sounding like he had Keith Moon in the studio to pound it out. It's interspersed with little keyboard washes and a rather feeble horn arrangement, neither of which complement the other confrontational aspects of the song.

## CRINGEMAKER

A TYPICAL Becker-esque couplet opens this blues based song. "Whatever happened to my College Belle/when did she turn into the wife from hell?" but despite the song's sleazy groove, it lacks a

decent hook and/or melody and never manages to climb out of its lowly furrow. Becker admitted he wanted it to be like an old Chess record where the guitarist found a good note "and just wailed away on it from beginning to end". Slim Harpo's 'I'm A King Bee' is the likeliest suspect, as evidenced by Becker muttering "Buzz awhile" over the guitar break at the end.

## GIRLFRIEND

'G IRLFRIEND' is downbeat and dowdy unlike the song's subject. Bob Sheppard's ragged sax solo suggests a man who is "at the dark outer limits of his soul" and who'd have thought that after all those cerebral subjects and far flung locations tackled by Steely Dan throughout the Seventies, the Nineties would see Walter Becker writing a song about an apathetic couch potato, including the lines "So I'm visualising a cute little bunny/with a fluffy white tail and long grey floppy ears."

## MY WATERLOO

A N UNINTERESTING lyric, featuring uninspired guitar and an unflattering vocal. For the most part during the 1996 tour, this was the only song from *Whack* which Becker played and virtually any of the other songs deserved inclusion more than this stinker.

## THIS MOODY BASTARD

MORE autobiography, perhaps for which Becker deserves full marks for honesty. Excluding 'Little Kawai' this is the nearest Becker gets to a ballad featuring a sinuous melody, but even then this ain't no lovestruck romantic singing his girlfriend's praises. He's been cast aside and is wallowing in self pity. Bob Sheppard's sax solo encapsulates that melancholy feeling.

## HAT TOO FLAT

IN WHICH Walter Becker goes in for a little musical slapstick, and succeeds with a story of extra-terrestrial job hunting. The friendly aliens have arrived from their distant star where life is very comfortable and leisurely, found jobs, picked up the language but still cannot gain acceptance due to their being fashion victims.

## LITTLE KAWAI

BECKER closes the album with an unashamed song of love to his sometime green haired son, Kawai, who occasionally joined the band on stage on the 1996 tour and who charmed and amused the road crew. Obviously the apple of his father's eye, Becker admitted that if he put the song on the album, it would earn him countless brownie points.

# COMPILATIONS/ MISCELLANEOUS

**B**ECAUSE STEELY DAN'S SEVENTIES OUTPUT WAS RELATIVELY LIMITED, their record company seemed determined to exploit this long hiatus in their career by surpassing their authorised studio albums with a tidal wave of *Greatest Hits* and *Best Of* compilations. At the last count, there were eight different compilations of Steely Dan available, not including 14 albums and CDs of early material.

# Greatest Hits

**ABC ABCD 616 November 1978, reissued as ABC ABCD 616; not released on CD**

**TRACKS:** Do It Again/Reelin' In The Years/My Old School/Bodhisattva/Show Biz Kids/East St. Louis Toodle-Oo/Rikki Don't Lose That Number/Pretzel Logic/Any Major Dude Will Tell You/Here At The Western World/Black Friday/Bad Sneakers/Doctor Wu/Haitian Divorce/Kid Charlemange/The Fez/Peg/Josie

**T**HE FIRST STEELY DAN COMPILATION ALBUM WAS A DOUBLE RELEASED in November 1978, containing eighteen songs, arranged in chronological order, selected by Becker and Fagen themselves. It sold extremely well (number 30 in America, number 41 in the UK), eventually gaining platinum status. There was just one new song, 'Here At The Western World', which was sandwiched between the *Pretzel Logic* and *Katy Lied* material. The front cover photograph was taken by Pete Turner, and the inside cover photo was taken during summer 1976 when Becker and Fagen were in Europe promoting *The Royal Scam*. Anton Corbijn captured them at Amsterdam's Hotel de L'Europe, and since the photograph was one of the duo's favourites, they decided to use it on the gatefold package. *Greatest Hits* was put together by Elliot Scheiner at A & R Studios in New York.

## HERE AT THE WESTERN WORLD

THIS 'bonus' track is described as an out-take from *The Royal Scam* sessions although it sounds more likely to be *Katy Lied* or indeed *Pretzel Logic*, as it supposedly features Jim Gordon on drums. On the *Citizen Steely Dan* box set Bernard Purdie is credited as the drummer. Michael Omartian plays a sublime piano melody while the background singers almost whisper behind Fagen's earnest voice on a song about an anything-goes whorehouse that is the choice for all the local dignataries and, indeed, is winning the competition with its main rival, the Lido. Becker and Fagen gave a second name check for a fan named Ruthie from Eugene, Oregon, whom they had previously mentioned in their *Volume Two* songbook under the guise of replying to fan mail.

# Gold

MCA MCF 3145, June 1982

**TRACKS:** Hey Nineteen/Green Earrings/Deacon Blues/Chain Lightning/FM (No Static At All)/Black Cow/King Of The World/Babylon Sisters

GOLD WAS THE FIRST VINYL COMPILATION TO BE RELEASED ON MCA BUT HAS absolutely nothing to recommend it, comprising eight songs featuring nothing at all from *Can't Buy A Thrill* or *Pretzel Logic*. The almost diaphanous cover artwork was again disappointing; there wasn't a photograph, an insert, a lyric sheet or a list of musicians. Money for old rope although the sound quality was as excellent as ever; Roger Nicholls, Wayne Yurgelun and Daniel Lazerus having transferred the original master tapes to digital format. *Gold* included one previously unreleased track...

## FM (NO STATIC AT ALL)

WHEN Becker and Fagen were asked by manager Irving Azoff to write a title song for a 1978 film about an LA radio station, they set out to come up with something which would "sound good with a big production coming out of movie theatre speakers". The track was built up from scratch, using the dreaded click track. Johnny Mandel was hired to do a string arrangement but this was overshadowed by a wonderful sneering vocal from Fagen, Pete Christlieb's near perfect sax interlude and Becker's meandering guitar phrases.

There are two different versions available: the original featured a Becker guitar solo, which, on later versions (*Gold* Expanded Edition, *Citizen Steely Dan* box set and *Remastered*) was replaced by an extended Christlieb saxophone solo. (*A Decade of Steely Dan* contains the original version.)

Naturally, AM radio stations were loath to play a record which plugged their rivals, and in an amazing display of ingenuity, took the 'A' from 'Aja', which was harmonically compatible, and edited it into the song for a more appropriate title. Despite the poor showing of the film, the single charted at number 22 in the US that summer.

---

NOVEMBER 1991 SAW THE RELEASE OF THE EXPANDED EDITION OF GOLD (MCA MCAD 10387), which added four more titles: 'Here At The Western World', 'Century's End', 'True Companion' and the live version of 'Bodhisattva' (from the B-side of 'Hey 19'.) Two of the extra tracks were, of course, Fagen solo compositions, and MCA would perhaps have been better advised to stick solely to Steely Dan material. Ever aware of achieving the best possible sound quality, Roger Nichols digitally recompiled the tapes at Soundworks West.

---

# A Decade Of Steely Dan

MCA DIDX August 1985; CD MCA MCAD 5570 (1985), DIDX 306 (1986)

**TRACKS:** FM (No Static At All)/Black Friday/Babylon Sisters/Deacon Blues/Bodhisattva/Hey Nineteen/Do It Again/Peg/Rikki Don't Lose That Number/Reelin' In The Years/East St. Louis Toodle-Oo/Kid Charlemange/My Old School/Bad Sneakers

---

A DECADE OF STEELY DAN WAS THE BAND'S FIRST CD COMPILATION, released in August 1985 but could not even come up to the standard set by its predecessor, featuring 14 songs in random order, a cover with all the appeal of a discarded paper bag, and zero sleeve notes. It did, however, have one slight redeeming feature, a full musicians listing for all songs which hitherto had not been available until *Aja*.

---

# Reeling In The Years –
# The Very Best Of
# Steely Dan

MCA MCADAN TV1, August 1985

**TRACKS:** Do It Again/Reelin' In The Years/My Old School/Bodhisattva/Show Biz Kids/Rikki Don't Lose That Number/Pretzel Logic/Any Major Dude Will Tell You/ Here At The Western World/Black Friday/Bad Sneakers/Doctor Wu/Haitian Divorce/Kid Charlemange/The Fez/Peg/Josie/Deacon Blues/Hey Nineteen/Babylon Sisters

# Do It Again –
# The Very Best Of
# Steely Dan

Telstar TCD 2279, September 1987

**TRACKS:** Rikki Don't Lose That Number /Reelin'/Kid Charlemange/Doctor Wu/FM/My Old School/The Fez/Do It Again/Pretzel Logic/Any Major Dude /Black Friday/Show Biz Kids/Peg/Haitian Divorce

NEXT CAME TWO BLATANT CASH-IN COMPILATIONS, *REELING IN THE YEARS – The Very Best Of Steely Dan* and *Do It Again – The Very Best Of Steely Dan*, basically TV advertised compilations. The MCA package depicted a blonde wearing sunglasses, sipping a fancy cocktail on the inside cover, with sleeve notes by Michael Gray; the Telstar version again offered no sleeve notes and, inexplicably, not one song from *Gaucho*.

# Remastered –
# The Best Of Steely Dan

**MCA MCD 10967, November 1993**

**TRACKS:** Reelin' In The Years/Rikki Don't Lose That Number/Peg/FM/Hey Nineteen/Deacon Blues/Black Friday/Bodhisattva/Do It Again/Haiatian Divorce/My Old School/Midnite Cruiser/Babylon Sisters/Kid Charlemagne/Dirty Work/Josie

CERTAINLY ONE OF THE BETTER COMPILATIONS, *REMASTERED* SHOWED an unusual bias towards material from *Can't Buy A Thrill* (songs that Fagen in particular, had been denouncing as "juvenilia"), with one quarter of the CD given over to Steely Dan's début. The front cover photo was of a sculpture based on Stonehenge entitled "Carhenge" by Jim Reinders which can be found two miles north of Alliance in Nebraska. The sleeve notes were written by John Tobler.

# Citizen Steely Dan
# 1972-1980

**MCA MCAD4 10981, December 1993**

THE LONG AWAITED BOX SET WAS A SERIOUS LET DOWN FOR ALL KNOWLEDGEABLE hard core Dan fans. No 'Dallas', no 'Sail The Waterway', no alternate versions, no out-takes and only one previously unreleased tidbit – an early demo version of 'Everyone's Gone To The Movies' featuring ex-Turtles Flo and Eddie on background vocals. The omnipresent 'FM', 'Here At The Western World' and 'Bodhisattva' were the token rare tracks. Aside from these slight interruptions, the running order started at the opening track on *Can't Buy A Thrill* and ran straight through to the final track on *Gaucho*.

Donald Fagen told *Q* Magazine at the time that... "Our shelves are pretty much empty," but quite frankly we don't believe him. The rarities are there, but Becker and Fagen haven't yet summoned the nerve to satisfy their fans' curiosity and desire for unreleased material. The pair did this before with the *Greatest Hits* album (only one new song) and it's about time they set aside this cussedness and offered fans the chance to make up their own minds about the standard of discarded product. Becker and Fagen also claimed that they did not believe that the fans' spirit was still with them for live gigs, but they have obviously realised since that this is not the case.

# The Steely Dan Story 1972-1980

MCA 088 112 407-2, November 2000

**A** **DOUBLE CD OF 33 PREVIOUSLY AVAILABLE REMASTERED TRACKS IN** chronological order. The sleeve featured tongue-in-cheek liner notes written by Becker and Fagen masquerading as a letter from Michael Phalen to Roger Nichols admitting to the theft of a missing *Aja* master tape and offering to share the $600 reward that Becker and Fagen had posted for its return. It also featured a classic never-before-seen photo of Becker and Fagen (circa-1977) posing above some Californian beach.

# EARLY MATERIAL
# The Early Years

LP Aero ML8901, 1983

**T**HE AVALANCHE OF PRE-STEELY DAN MATERIAL COMMENCED IN **1983** WITH *The Early Years*. As well as writing the sleevenotes Kenny Vance compiled the whole project including a cover showing a dog-eared Marty Kupersmith photograph of Becker and Fagen in Jay & The Americans' Brill Building office. Their "rickety atonal upright" on which they ostensibly composed songs for Jay and The Americans is just visible behind Becker's shoulder.

The ten tracks on *The Early Years* were a revelation when first issued since Becker and Fagen had been referring to 'Brain Tap Shuffle', 'Let George Do It' and 'Take It Out On Me' in interviews for years; in some cases gloating because the journalist in question was unlikely to have ever heard these songs. At last people were able to hear and judge for themselves. Despite their inevitable initial opposition to its release, *The Early Years* is a worthwhile purchase for any Steely Dan fan who wants to visit Becker and Fagen's weird pre-Dan world.

After *The Early Years*, several unauthorised recordings, containing early demos, appeared on the market at cheap prices. Each contained a random selection of songs from the 1968-71 period featuring numerous duplications.

## BRAIN TAP SHUFFLE

A SORT OF acid-inspired dance track which features both Becker and Fagen sharing the lead vocal and Keith Thomas' high background vocals adding a certain hallucinatory quality. The nearest Becker and Fagen ever came to psychedelia.

## COME BACK BABY

A STRAIGHTFORWARD song looking for reconciliation and a cry for mercy. John Mazzi makes the first of his three able guest appearances on drums, Dias' guitar solo sounds somewhat harsh and Fagen's voice is much more to the fore.

## DON'T LET ME IN

THIS sees Becker and Fagen full of self-denial and negativity and was later covered by a band called Sneaker. The producer was Jeff Baxter who still loves the song and was proposing to do a version of it himself a few years ago. Kenny Vance assists on background vocals; Becker's bass rumbles heavily.

## OLD REGIME

A JAUNTY song on which Keith Thomas sings weird lyrics as if he's fully aware of what it's all about, which is most doubtful. It could be about America's enormous problems with the war in Vietnam and a fear of being drafted. In 1968 President Johnson stood down and Richard Nixon was elected, but despite peace talks the war and the wholesale slaughter of US soldiers continued.

## BROOKLYN

FAGEN'S vocal is mournful but doesn't sound all that convincing. The organ simmers away beneath the surface on this long and sad reflection about a former neighbour. Elliott Randall guests on guitar. The *Can't Buy A Thrill* version is far superior.

## MOCK TURTLE SONG

BECKER and Fagen very cleverly adapted Lewis Carroll's poem to music and the former sings with panache. Denny Dias' guitar solo is adroit and demonstrates his wonderful touch on the instrument – his percussion is almost as effective.

## SOUL RAM

'SOUL Ram' details a number of sexual perversions: masturbation, anal sex, sadism and naturally the use of vibrators. This was the song in which they referred to Steely Dan long before they decided to use it as the name for their band. Note the lack of guitars.

## I CAN'T FUNCTION

ANOTHER shared vocal on a song about impotence which finds Fagen playing saxophone of all things. (Inspired by Charlie Parker both Becker and Fagen at some point tried playing the saxophone but neither succeeded). Becker's bass and vocal are confidently administered.

## YELLOW PERIL

DONALD Fagen's Oriental obsession rears its head. Originally called 'Finah Minah From China' this basic demo seems to detail the end of a conflict as caused by some earth shattering music. There's no bass on the song; Becker switches to guitar and Fagen's piano is prevalent. Kenny Vance plays a hi-hat but credits himself with "drums".

## LET GEORGE DO IT

A FINE ending is provided by this , which is actually the title of a 1940 George Formby film, but it's questionable whether Becker and Fagen knew that or whether they would be amused or interested enough to write a song based on it if they did. Keith Thomas provides his best vocal, with funky piano from Fagen, and some great guitar from Denny Dias. Among other unfathomable lyrics, it contains a reference to Avogadro's number.

# Catalyst (The Original Recordings 1968-1971)

LP: Thunderbolt 1994 | CD: Magnum 502, 1995

CATALYST WAS BY FAR THE BEST OF ALL THE SUBSEQUENT DEMO RELEASES, since it was a double CD set, featuring all the available 28 songs in one package (including the ten tracks from *The Early Years*.) A hitherto-unreleased song ('Undecided') was acquired from some nefarious source. However, the compilers were unable to trace versions of 'Any Way You Want It', 'Mr. Lyle' and 'One Ticket To L.A.' which remain unreleased (to date).

---

## SUN MOUNTAIN

'SUN MOUNTAIN' is a simple piano and voice demo with an uncomplicated lyric – the sort of thing that Becker and Fagen might have asked David Palmer to take a shot at if they'd recorded it for *Can't Buy A Thrill*. The more fully realised group version on Disc Two is sung by Kenny Vance and is a fine version (albeit in very poor quality) of what was a good song that could have been developed into an excellent track.

## BARRYTOWN

ANOTHER piano and voice demo. Fagen doesn't sound at all confident being laid bare in this way, especially on the higher parts.

## TAKE IT OUT ON ME

A TAWDRY tale, regarding self-abuse and sado-masochism, which Becker and Fagen often mentioned in Steely Dan interviews.

## THE CAVES OF ALTAMIRA

A JAZZED-UP piano part, an extra verse, and Fagen singing in a Lou Reed-style monotone with Becker joining in on the chorus. 'The Caves...' is about a kid's escape from the real world. When he returns in later life things have changed for the worse; the secret's out and it's now a major tourist attraction.

## CHARLIE FREAK

FAGEN is in good form on piano, otherwise it's pretty much the same as the *Pretzel Logic* version.

## YOU GO WHERE I GO

A CLAUSTROPHOBIC relationship story similar to what Sting and The Police would later explore on 'Every Breath You Take'.

## ANY WORLD THAT I'M WELCOME TO

BECKER plays bass on this demo, but the chorus sounds forced. The duo initially intended this to be sung by a female but when they came to cut the song for *Katy Lied* it had the considerable benefit of Mike McDonald's tubes.

## A LITTLE WITH SUGAR

A POSSIBLE pocket autobiography in which Fagen gets as passionate as he's able to towards the end. Vance sings backup vocals.

## ANDROID WAREHOUSE

'ANDROID Warehouse' features a rhythmic piano, and percussion with Becker late on the vocal on the chorus.

## MORE TO COME

A JOINT vocal, slapped percussion and occasional falsetto vocals from Thomas who name checks William Burroughs and his heroin habit.

## PARKER'S BAND

A ROUGH version, featuring token percussion and awkward harmony vocals from Becker.

## OH WOW IT'S YOU

NOT A straightforward love song but another of Becker and Fagen's typically idiosyncratic takes on romance.

## STONE PIANO

AN EXTREMELY enigmatic and confusing number.

## ROARING OF THE LAMB

STEELY Dan did try to record this song as one of their first two recordings.

## THIS SEAT'S BEEN TAKEN

A SONG about loneliness and longing, this one could be an outtake from the duo's list of compositions for the Peter Locke movie *You Gotta Walk It Like You Talk It*.

## IDA LEE

'IDA LEE', about a party girl, contains a line which Becker and Fagan would later use on 'Josie' ("hooters and the hats").

## UNDECIDED

A GROUP version with Keith Thomas on vocals, featuring the contrasting lyrics, "I love you, go away/I hate you, no please stay."

# LIVE ALBUMS

## The New York Rock And Soul Revue – Live At The Beacon

Giant 7599-24 423.2, 1991

**F**AGEN MADE HIS REAPPEARANCE ON STAGE IN SEPTEMBER 1989 AT Manhattan's Lone Star Roadhouse. It was a low key deal – a tribute to the songwriting team of Bert Berns and Jerry Ragavoy who had written such classics as 'Piece Of My Heart', 'Time Is On My Side', 'Twist And Shout', and 'Everybody Needs Somebody To Love.' Ragavoy actually turned up and was presented with a memento of the occasion by Fagen, who was more than a little irritated by the inevitable requests for Steely Dan numbers and bluntly refused to sing at all. However, as the months and indeed the year progressed, Fagen's attitude relaxed and he played with a wide variety of names including Dr John, Rickie Lee Jones and Al Kooper. He eventually eased himself back into a vocal role with versions of Gamble and Huff's 'Drowning In The Sea Of Love' and Bob Dylan's 'Down Along The Cove' (from *John Wesley Harding*.)

About six months after the Lone Star gig, Fagen and wife-to-be Libby Titus decided that there was scope for a more substantial role for the Rock and Soul Revue and a one-off, sold-out gig was arranged at the Beacon Theatre in April 1990 featuring Michael McDonald, Patti Austin, Phoebe Snow, and Jeff Young and Curious George. In March 1991 the show performed again on consecutive nights, both of which were recorded and released on CD later that year. This time the line-up included Boz Scaggs, Phoebe Snow, Michael McDonald and Charles Brown, each performing a few carefully selected songs. At this stage Walter Becker was not involved.

The Steely Dan element was still limited, although Fagen performed 'Chain Lightning', 'Pretzel Logic', 'Home At Last', and 'Black Friday', but the latter two songs didn't make it onto the CD. Fagen and Elliott Scheiner also rearranged the running order to make it flow better.

The following year Fagen took the Revue out on the road for a three-week, 12-date tour, with Chuck Jackson replacing Charles Brown. Each guest performed a favourite or two from their own repertoire as well as the designated soul tunes. Becker went along, and surprised fans with his version of the song 'Mary, Mary' which was usually introduced with the words: "The Monkees recorded this, but we'll do it anyway." There was no reservation about adding yet more Steely Dan songs to the list: 'Green Earrings', 'Josie', 'Deacon Blues', and 'My Old School.' The rapturous reception to the opening chords of each Steely Dan tune was such that it convinced Becker and Fagen to return a year later to do a tour of exclusively Steely Dan material and what's more actually call themselves Steely Dan. Their manager Craig Fruin had obviously been busy waving dollar bills in front of them to encourage the re-adoption of their Burroughs-inspired moniker.

## MADISON TIME – KNOCK ON WOOD

STEVE Cropper and Eddie Floyd knocked off such a great song in 'Knock On Wood' that it would be difficult to imagine such a great combination of voices making a hash of it. Mike McDonald starts off this natural show opener, with Phoebe Snow joining in. Jeff Young plays the organ solo.

## GREEN FLOWER STREET

FAGEN plays the melodica on the intro of this Oriental romance, but it sounds a little thin against the rest of the big band.

## SHAKEY GROUND – AT LAST

LINCOLN Schleifer's bass takes the spotlight on a Temptations tune which Snow recorded on her 1976 album *It Looks Like Snow*. She really goes for broke, yelling and screaming with real emotion, with musical director Larry de Bari solo-ing.

On 'At Last' which follows, it sounds like she's trying to shred her vocal cords again.

## LONELY TEARDROPS

WHILE Jackie Wilson lay in a coma in hospital his hit was given another triumphant airing by Mike McDonald, whose voice transcends human capabilities.

## DROWNING IN THE SEA OF LOVE

ANOTHER great song, but this time Boz Scaggs doesn't get the funk and it can't compete with Joe Simon's original. Drew Zingg takes the guitar solo.

## DRIFTIN' BLUES

AGEING special guest Charles Brown sang a version of this remarkable composition written when he was just twelve years old.

## CHAIN LIGHTNING

ALONG with 'Black Friday' this blues based number from *Katy Lied* was chosen by Fagen as one of the first Dan tunes worthy of live experiment. And who'd have thought you would ever hear a solo by a man imitating the sound of a trumpet on a Becker and/or Fagen record?

## GROOVIN'

THE YOUNG Rascals' all time classic '67 Summer of Love hit is lazy, warm and relaxing, and this live version almost succeeds in transporting the audience into that Central Park sunshine on a memorable Sunday afternoon.

## MINUTE BY MINUTE

THE TITLE track and a Top 20 hit from the 1979 Doobie Brothers album. The horn section and Drew Zingg go hand in hand all the way.

## PEOPLE GOT TO BE FREE

ANOTHER Rascals hit provides the opportunity for all the artists to be brought out on to the stage for a rowdy sing-along finish.

## PRETZEL LOGIC

A MARVELLOUS finish with Fagen and McDonald reliving their halcyon days from 1974 when they used to play this together on stage. McDonald sounds like he's holding back Drew Zingg.

# Alive In America

**CD: Giant 74321 25691-2, October 1995**

STEELY DAN'S FIRST OFFICIAL LIVE ALBUM – RECORDED ON THEIR 1993 AND 1994 tours – was released in May 1995. Although every show was recorded on both tours, the final selection of cuts showed a heavy bias towards the 1994 dates, with eight drawn from the second outing. The Detroit show on August 27, 1994 provided four of the 11 songs alone.

Becker and Fagen had termed the 1993 band 'The All-New Fresh For 1993 Steely Dan Orchestra' and in 1994, in the wake of the box set, this became 'The Citizen Steely Dan Orchestra'. The only personnel changes were Swedish guitarist (ex-Blood Sweat And Tears) Georg Wadenius replacing Drew Zingg and Dennis Chambers replacing Peter Erskine on drums. Apparently Chambers had been their original choice for the 1993 tour but he had other commitments that summer. The other players were Warren Bernhardt on keyboards, Tom Barney on bass, Bill Ware on percussion, a three-man horn section and three female background singers.

For the set list, Becker and Fagen dropped 'IGY', 'Teahouse On The Tracks', 'Countermoon', 'Book of Liars' and 'Fall Of '92' and in '94 added 'Kid Charlemagne', 'Down In The Bottom', 'Sign In Stranger', 'Hard Up Case' and 'Aja'. Fagen now sported a grey, scraggly half beard and Becker was growing his hair again.

*Alive In America* was produced by Fagen alone and he and Roger Nichols used digital edits and crossfades in order to create the impression that it had "all happened on one glorious night", with each song being arranged to allow maximum space for soloing. Early rumours indicating that the live offering would be a double were quashed with only a disappointing single CD supposedly representing a 20-plus song show which lasted for two and a half hours. The cover featured a still from the classic 1932 horror movie *The Mummy*.

Opening with a version of 'Babylon Sisters', recorded at St. Petersburg, Florida on the first date of the 1994 tour, Dennis Chambers does a good impersonation of the Purdie shuffle. Other highlights were a new arrangement of 'Reelin' In The Years' with its keyboard intro and sax-driven hook, a 1993 rendition of 'Third World Man' featuring musical director Drew Zingg doing his astounding, carbon copy Larry Carlton impression and a nine-minute 'Aja' complete with drum solo. Becker and Fagen were seemingly unaware of the disdain in which drum solos are nowadays held – on the 1996 tour two drum solos were featured within the first fifteen minutes.

For 'Peg' Georg Wadenius had the thankless task of replicating Jay Graydon's solo. Ultimately, it sounds a little empty and could have benefited from Michael McDonald's voice on the chorus. Another disappointment was 'Sign In Stranger' which chugs along with prominent vibes and new lyrics on the bridge; Warren Berhnardt taking Griffin's piano solo. 'Book Of Liars' (Becker's only vocal on the album) was still to be released when this live version was recorded and it was indeed a brave and bold move to debut unfamiliar solo material among all the Steely Dan classics.

# OUTSIDE PROJECTS

**B**ECKER AND FAGEN HAVE STRICTLY CONTROLLED STEELY DAN'S CATALOGUE thus far and there is virtually nothing in the way of rare B-sides, non-album tracks or alternate versions available. All their singles were backed by tracks from the relevant album (on one occasion the record company used the same song twice) and the only interesting and collectable issues consist of promo seven-inch jukebox EPs for *Countdown To Ecstasy* and *Pretzel Logic*. The former was a three song picture sleeve release containing 'My Old School', 'Pearl Of The Quarter' and 'King Of The World', while the latter was quadrophonic, also with a picture sleeve and featured 'With A Gun', 'Rikki Don't Lose That Number', 'Barrytown' and 'Pretzel Logic.' The Plus Fours 12" single which came out in the UK on ABC in January 1978 was most welcome, since it coupled 'Do It Again' and 'Haitian Divorce' with the thoroughly excellent 'Dallas' and 'Sail The Waterway'.

Down the years Becker and Fagen have permitted their considerable talents to be viewed on a number of outside projects, whether as musicians, songwriters and/or producers. Their first experience of a professional recording studio was Terence Boylan's *Alias Boona* album, recorded in 1969 at the Hit Factory in New York. Becker and Fagen played bass and guitar and piano and organ respectively. A year later they were credited with arranging horns and strings on four songs on Jay & The Americans' *Capture The Moment* album and Kenny Vance succeeded in getting his producer friend Richard Perry to offer Barbra Streisand the duo's composition 'I Mean To Shine.' However, the pair were ungrateful and thereafter disowned the song saying that Perry "changed the lyrics and the melody and left out the bridge".

The film, *You Gotta Walk It Like You Talk It, Or You'll Lose That Beat* starred Zalman King and Richard Pryor. Upon its release in 1971 the critics gave it such a panning that its run in the Manhattan movie theatres was restricted to just a few days. All Becker and Fagen's songs followed the same theme and only one was previously unreleased – a demo of 'Everyone's Gone To The Movies'. Steely Dan's first single, 'Dallas', was omitted, as was 'Sail The Waterway' (neither yet to appear on CD). Fans were entitled to ask why unreleased gems such as 'Heartbreak Souvenir', 'Kulee Baba', 'Shanghai Breakdown', 'Were You Blind That Day?' 'Mr. Sam', and 'Gullywater' had not been included.

When a hard-rocking band from Texas named Navasota recorded Becker and Fagen's song 'Canyon Ladies' in 1972, it was presumably written during their stint as staff writers at ABC, since it's impossible to imagine Steely Dan recording it. The banshee yell at the start and the gravelly-voiced lead singer contrast sharply with the horns and strings arranged by Becker and Fagen.

In 1973 another hard rocker, John Kay, ex-lead singer of Steppenwolf, cut the song 'Giles Of The River', which was considerably mellower than the aforementioned 'Canyon Ladies', another composition which Fagen later dismissed by saying that "you could tell it wasn't a very good song just by the title."

Thomas Jefferson Kaye was an associate from the duo's Jay and The Americans period, and when Gary Katz produced a couple of his solo albums in 1973 and 1974, Becker and Fagen played on both. The latter album, *First Grade*, featured a crack band including Dean Parks, Michael Omartian, Jim Gordon and, surprisingly, Dusty Springfield on background vocals. Two excellent Becker and Fagen songs were included, the spacious 'American Lovers' which closed side one and 'Jones' – a jazz term for a drug habit – which opened side two.

Becker and Fagen then retreated into their shells for a few years, Fagen reemerging in 1977 to play on Terence Boylan's eponymous album and Poco's *Indian Summer*. A year later he played piano on Marc Jordan's *Mannequin* album, another Gary Katz production. Also in 1978, the pair wrote a song called 'Rapunzel', based on Burt Bacharach and Hal David's 'In The Land Of Make Believe' as recorded by Dionne Warwick. It was a particular favourite of Fagen's, who decided it would be nice to adapt for an out and out jazz album. The song was recorded by the Pete Christlieb/Warne Marsh Quintet, Becker and Fagen produced it and their friend from Village Recorders, Dick LaPalm, suggested the title 'Apogee.'

In 1978 Woody Herman's Big Band devoted a whole side of an album *Chick, Donald, Walter and Woodrow* to Fagen/Becker compositions. Side one featured Chick Corea's 'Suite For A Hot Band', while on side two the Thundering Herd did big band versions of 'Deacon Blues', 'Green Earrings', 'Kid Charlemagne', 'I Got The News', 'Aja', and 'FM'. Becker and Fagen were well pleased and attended a few of the sessions to show their appreciation.

1979 saw Dr Strut, a Motown band featuring Tim Weston (The Stafford Boy from *Countdown To Ecstasy*), recording an instrumental Becker and Fagen song, 'Canadian Star', on their debut album. It's an absolutely divine song which Steely Dan had attempted to record but which they had consigned to the rejects bin. Its slow and melodic intro opens out into a panoramic guitar hook and slowly builds to a crescendo of horns. Hearing a Steely Dan version, complete with lyrics, would be something.

Donald Fagen appeared playing synth on the title track to Rickie Lee Jones' *Pirates* album and sang background vocals on an obscure album by Far Cry, produced by Elliott Scheiner, called *The More Things Change*. After their split, Fagen was asked to write a song for the animated film *Heavy Metal*. His contribution was basically an instrumental with a few harmony vocals named after a spaceship called the "True Companion". It's an atmospheric piece, with Steve Khan, who was obviously Fagen's guitar player of choice at that time, contributing some very fine acoustic guitar before an even better electric solo. Invariably when Gary Katz was involved in a project he would ask Fagen if he wanted to contribute in some way. The two albums Katz produced for a group called Eye To Eye (*Eye To Eye*, *Shakespeare Stole My Baby*) featured Fagen on keyboards (along with numerous other Steely Dan session types).

Robbie Robertson asked Fagen to contribute a song for the Martin Scorsese and Robert de Niro film *King Of Comedy* (1980). He offered another mainly instrumental piece called 'The Finer Things', performed by saxophonist David Sanborn, which had been left off *The Nightfly* a year earlier.

In 1983 Hal Wilner put together a tribute to Thelonious Monk entitled *That's The Way I Feel Now* wherein a variety of artists covered their favourite Monk composition. Fagen was a fan of Steve Khan's *Evidence* album, and suggested they do something together. While most of the other artists were covering medium or up tempo numbers Khan advocated doing one of Monk's ballads to show how beautiful his writing could be. They chose 'Reflections' and their version later appeared on the soundtrack album to *Arthur 2: On The Rocks*.

That same year Gary Katz part-produced an album for Diana Ross, *Ross*, to which Fagen contributed 'Love Will Make It Right', a synth-dominated song about a secret love affair between two close friends whose respective partners haven't yet realized what is going on.

After Fagen had been to see a show called *The Gospel At Colonus*, based on Sophocles Oedipus at Colonus, and came away highly impressed, he persuaded Daniel Lazerus to see it and co-producing an album of the production with Bob Telson at Clinton Studios. Also in 1984 keyboardist Greg Phillinganes who had been featured extensively on *The Nightfly*, did a version of 'Lazy Nina'. Phillinganes voice, however, was pretty uninspiring and the lack of guitars leave the listener unfulfilled. The same song was later recorded by a Canadian group, Monkey House with Fagen giving their version a ringing endorsement.

The inevitable rumours about a Steely Dan reunion started in 1986 when Becker and Fagen both appeared on ex-model Rosie Vela's debut album, *Zazu*. Inevitably it was a Gary Katz production which brought them back into the studio together, with Fagen playing on seven of the album's nine songs. Fagen wrote the title song for the jazz-fusion band Yellowjackets 1986 album, *Shades*. Ten years later, hot session drummer Ricky Lawson joined Steely Dan on their 1996 Art Crimes tour.

Named after a Becker/Fagen character from 'Glamour Profession', The Hoops McCann Band followed in the footsteps of Woody Herman and recorded an entire album of Steely Dan songs. It consisted of eight tunes played by ex-Dan guest players like Chuck Findley, Jerome Richardson and Paul Humphrey with Joe Roccisano conducting the band and handling the arrangements.

Michael Franks became separately linked with Becker and Fagen, thanking the latter for an unspecified reason in an extensive list of credits on his 1987 album *The Camera Never Lies*. Three years later Becker produced three songs on Franks' *Blue Pacific* album.

In 1988, while still in the midst of his creative block, Fagen wrote the score to *Bright Lights, Big City* produced by his cousin Mark Rosenberg. The film was based on Jay McInerney's yuppie novel and a single (Fagen's first since 'Ruby Baby') 'Century's End', co-written with Timothy Meher, featured that squeaky synth sound which characterises late Eighties Fagen. Despite a video being made to aid in promotion, it failed to chart in the US or the UK.

Fagen was credited with co-writing 'A New Standard By Which To Measure Infamy' with William Burroughs on his *Dead City Radio* CD. The track is just 1'47" in duration and even that is too long. Burroughs opines incomprehensibly and Fagen provides the music and effects which are almost non-existent. For hardened Dan fans only.

Manhattan Transfer covered Fagen's composition 'Confide In Me' on their *The Offbeat Of Avenues* in 1991. The song was about someone offering a friend with a substance problem comfort to get through the terrible withdrawal process. In this sumptuous Mervyn Warren arrangement, Mike Finnigan's brief jazzy Hammond solo prefaces Jamie Glaser's guitar solo and the highly trained Transfer voices compete with Jeff Porcaro's beats in one of his last session appearances. Fagen released his demo of the song on the edit-only version of the 'Tomorrow's Girls' CD single.

Based on the David Mamet play, *Glengarry Glen Ross* was a film about greedy real estate developers, starring Al Pacino and Jack Lemmon. Fagen's contribution to the soundtrack album was 'Blue Lou', performed by The Joe Roccisano Orchestra, a seven-minute instrumental inspired by his work and friendship with Lou Marini (renowned for his part in The Blues Brothers band) who features on alto.

Jennifer Warnes recorded a version of Fagen and Marcelle Clements' then unreleased song 'Big Noise, New York' on her album *The Hunter* in 1992. A lazy sax captures the feeling of a once vibrant city, but now her partner's gone and the cold streets are merely mirrors of her feelings of emptiness. Fagen sang background vocals too, but you can barely hear him above Frank Floyd. The mighty Robben Ford stars on guitar. Fagen later released his own version on the 'Trans-Island Skyway' single.

# WALTER BECKER PRODUCTIONS

**1985**  China Crisis – Flaunt The Imperfection

**1987**  Fra Lippo Lippi – Light And Shade

**1989**  China Crisis – Diary Of A Hollow Horse

Rickie Lee Jones – Flying Cowboys

*(Becker receives a co-writing credit on 'The Horses')*

**1990**  Michael Franks – Blue Pacific

## Jazz productions for Triloka:

**1991**  Andy Laverne – Pleasureseekers

**1991**  Leeann Ledgerwood – You Wish

**1991**  Jeff Beal – Objects in the Mirror

**1991**  Bob Bangerter – Looking on the Bright Side

**1992**  Jeremy Steig – Jigsaw

**1992**  Dave Kikoski – Persistent Dreams

**1993**  Andy Laverne – Double Standards

## Jazz productions for Windham Hill:

**1991**  Bob Sheppard Tell Tale Signs

**1993**  Lost Tribe – Lost Tribe

**1993**  John Beasley – Cauldron

**1993**  John Beasley – A Change of Heart

# Index

A Little With Sugar 68
Aja 33
Almost Gothic 42
Android Warehouse 68
Any Major Dude Will Tell You 19
Any World (That I'm Welcome To) 25,67

Babylon Sisters 37
Bad Sneakers 23
Barrytown 19,67
Black Cow 33
Black Friday 23
Blues Beach 45
Bodhisattva 13
Book Of Liars 56
Boston Rag, The 14
Brain Tap Shuffle 65
Brooklyn 65
Brooklyn (Owes The Charmer Under Me) 11

Caves Of Altamira, The 29,67
Chain Lightning 25,71
Change Of The Guard 11
Charlie Freak 21,67
Come Back Baby 65
Counter Moon 52
Cousin Dupree 42
Cringemaker 57

Daddy Don't Live In That New York City No More 24

Deacon Blues 34
Dirty Work 9
Do It Again 9
Don't Let Me In 65
Don't Take Me Alive 29
Down In The Bottom 56
Dr Wu 24
Driftin' Blues 70
Drowning In The Sea Of Love 70

East St Louis Toodle-Oo 20
Everyone's Gone To The Movies 24
Everything Must Go 46
Everything You Did 30

FM (No Static At All) 60
Fez, The 29
Fire In The Hole 11
Florida Room 53

Gaslighting Abbie 41
Gaucho 38
Girlfriend 57
Glamour Profession 38
Godwhacker 45
Goodbye Look, The 50
Green Book 46
Green Earrings 29
Green Flower Street 49,70
Groovin' 71

Haitian Divorce 30
Hard Up Case 57
Hat Too Flat 58

Here At The Western World 60
Hey Nineteen 37
Home At Last 35

I.G.Y. (What A Beautiful World) 48
I Can't Function 66
I Got The News 35
Ida Lee 68

Jack Of Speed 42
Janie Runaway 42
Josie 35
Junkie Girl 56

Kid Charlemagne 28
King Of The World 16
Kings 9

Last Mail, The 45
Let George Do It 66
Little Kawai 58
Lonely Teardrops 70
Lucky Henry 57
Lunch With Gina 46

Madison Time/ Knock On Wood 70
Maxine 49
Midnight Cruiser 10
Minute By Minute 71
Mock Turtle Song 65
Monkey In Your Soul 21
More To Come 68
My Old School 15
My Rival 39

| | |
|---|---|
| My Waterloo | 57 |

| | |
|---|---|
| Negative Girl | 43 |
| New Frontier | 49 |
| Night By Night | 19 |
| Nightfly, The | 50 |

| | |
|---|---|
| Oh Wow It's You | 68 |
| Old Regime | 65 |
| On The Dunes | 53 |
| Only A Fool Would Say That | 10 |

| | |
|---|---|
| Parker's Band | 20,68 |
| Pearl Of The Quarter | 16 |
| Peg | 34 |
| People Got To Be Free | 71 |
| Pixeleen | 46 |
| Pretzel Logic | 21,71 |

| | |
|---|---|
| Razor Boy | 13 |
| Reelin' In The Years | 10 |
| Rikki Don't Lose That Number | 18 |
| Roaring Of The Lamb | 68 |
| Rose Darling | 24 |
| Royal Scam, The | 31 |
| Ruby Baby | 49 |

| | |
|---|---|
| Shakey Ground – At Last | 70 |
| Show Biz Kids | 14 |
| Sign In Stranger | 29 |
| Slang Of Ages | 46 |
| Snowbound | 53 |
| Soul Ram | 66 |
| Springtime | 52 |
| Stone Piano | 68 |

| | |
|---|---|
| Sun Mountain | 67 |
| Surf And/Or Die | 56 |

| | |
|---|---|
| Take It Out On Me | 67 |
| Teahouse On The Tracks | 54 |
| Things I Miss The Most | 45 |
| This Moody Bastard | 58 |
| This Seat's Been Taken | 68 |
| Third World Man | 39 |
| Through With Buzz | 20 |
| Throw Back The Little Ones | 26 |
| Time Out Of Mind | 39 |
| Tomorrow's Girls | 53 |
| Trans-Island Skyway | 52 |
| Turn That Heartbeat Over Again | 11 |
| Two Against Nature | 41 |

| | |
|---|---|
| Undecided | 68 |

| | |
|---|---|
| Walk Between Raindrops | 50 |
| West Of Hollywood | 43 |
| What A Shame About Me | 41 |
| With A Gun | 21 |

| | |
|---|---|
| Yellow Peril | 66 |
| You Go Where I Go | 67 |
| Your Gold Teeth | 14 |
| Your Gold Teeth II | 25 |